An Idol Unmasked

An Idol Unmasked

A Faith Perspective on Money

Peter Selby

DARTON · LONGMAN + TODD

First published in 2014 by
Darton, Longman and Todd Ltd
1 Spencer Court
140 – 142 Wandsworth High Street
London SW18 4JJ

ISBN 978-0-232-53111-4

A catalogue record for this book is available from the British Library

Phototypeset by Kerrypress Ltd, Luton, Bedfordshire
Printed and bound in Great Britain by Bell & Bain, Glasgow

For
HARVEY GUTHRIE

and in grateful memory of
JOHN AUSTIN BAKER

Mentors   Teachers   Friends

Contents

Preface

In the decade and a half that has elapsed since I wrote *Grace and Mortgage* – and indeed in the five years since the book was reissued in response to the financial crisis of 2008 and all that has followed from it – nothing has happened to inspire confidence that fundamental lessons have been learned. There has been a great deal of activity and debate: most notably there has been much discussion of what might be the regulatory changes that would prevent such a crisis from happening again. On the other hand some have for good reason suspected that *regulation* would not bear the burden that was expected of it unless there was deep change in the underlying corporate *culture*; without that, some traders and bankers would continue to direct their enormous financial ingenuity towards finding ways around any regulations.

Partly because of that suspicion, but partly perhaps in the hope of avoiding further regulation of their activity, the financial sector has adopted 'culture' as one of its most fashionable terms, and most corporate bodies would wish it to be known that they are determined to change their 'culture' for the better. Their hope is that what were at best imprudent and at worst immoral activities that had precipitated the crisis of 2008, and in the process done enormous damage to the level of confidence in the financial sector, would be prevented by being very evidently contrary to the approved way of behaving.

However, several commissions and reorganisations later, and with much new mission-statement composition behind us, the level of distrust remains high. There are many reasons for the culture of blame which persists, but there is no doubt about what is a principal cause of this distrust. To put it very simply, in a period where some of the poorest have suffered greatly from the policies which governments have instituted to restore the world economy and where even those who would not think of themselves as poor have experienced a jolt to their expectation of rising living standards, conspicuous salaries and headline bonuses have continued unabated in the financial sector.

While we may consider that the opening question following my Hugh Price Hughes lecture in 2013, 'Why have no bankers gone to prison?', is somewhat harsh, and while we may indeed sympathise with the second questioner who asked, 'What did anyone ever learn by going to prison?', the sense of injustice is palpable. After all, 'money talks', and in this case the message conveyed by the figures seems to be that while something went wrong and a few people sailed rather close to the wind, the rewards available in that sector are fully justified and indeed absolutely necessary if the 'talent' required for putting things right is going to be recruited. Leaving aside the obvious question whether the talent that was so evidently involved in creating the mess is the talent we need to get us out of it, the level of anger at the high rewards provided for failure is surely understandable, and the Occupy protests struck a chord with a far wider constituency than those who would normally sympathise with activities of that kind.

So if money continues to talk, and to talk in that way, maybe money itself needs some examining: is there something about money which makes it talk in that way, and prevents that kind of talk from being silenced? After the 2008 crisis was well under way, an eminent person wittily suggested that I should write a follow-up to *Grace and Mortgage* and call it *I Told You So*. It is not just the appalling smugness of such a title that rules it out; the fact is that there were far too many gaps in the argument of that book, far too many aspects left unexamined, for me to make such an extravagant claim. That book was overwhelmingly to do with debt, and while debt is a crucial aspect of the crisis that has overtaken humanity it is in many ways a symptom. Debt is, after all, mostly computed in money – if I borrow my neighbour's lawnmower I am duty bound to return it, but that isn't usually called a 'debt'. More important, it is not just that debt is an issue about money but, as will become very clear as the argument of this book proceeds, by far the greatest proportion of our money is in fact debt.

So during the intervening years I have become preoccupied with the issue of money, what it has become and what it now is and does and the language, if you will, that it now talks. In that pursuit I am far from original: many have been working on this theme for far longer than I; some of their writings are referred to later, and there is far more now available than I have had the time or the ability fully to understand. There have been small, often brilliant, always admirably persistent, organisations making the point that money is behind most issues of justice and sustainability. Top of the league among my acquaintance – which is not to say anything negative about others whom I may not know – is the Christian Council for Monetary Justice (http://ccmj.org.uk) and its remarkable Chair, Peter Challen; their gathering together of literature, argument and friends in solidarity has been exceptional, particularly since they carry on with this even when neither corporate life nor academy nor church pays them anywhere near the attention they deserve.

In more recent years, it has been my privilege to be associated with St Paul's Institute (http://stpaulsinstitute.org.uk), the agency set up by the Chapter of St Paul's Cathedral to seek to be in dialogue with those who work in the field of finance in the City of London. Distinguished work has gone on under its auspices, much of it through the creativity of its successive directors, and my association with that body began with an invitation to speak at an event and then write a series of articles for the Institute website. That invitation has required me to think, discuss and read, and I am enormously grateful for all that my association with the Institute has given me, particularly during the most recent period when I have been allowed to be part of the team which has been leading it, alongside Canon Mark Oakley, the Chancellor of St Paul's, David Rouch, and the Institute's Manager, Robert Gordon. The events we have been able to organise have been enormously stimulating, and have without doubt advanced the conversation that needs to happen. As colleagues they have been enormously patient with my riding of hobby horses, and have been kind enough to permit me to use in this book, in adapted form, much of the material that appeared first in those website articles.

For this book is in effect my attempt, with their encouragement and that of others, to draw together the threads of disparate pieces of thinking and writing that I have produced over the years, in the hope of making out of them a more sustained argument. It is not, therefore, a 'collection of essays', but it does make use, in adapted form, of lectures and other writings that have appeared before. I have been grateful to the following who have kindly granted me permission to use material which they first published:

The publishers of the *Church Times* (www.churchtimes. co.uk), for permission to repeat points made in a number of articles which they have been kind enough to commission over the years, and in particular to include an extract from my article 'Lament for Octavia Hill', which first appeared in the *Church Times* of 19 April 2011.

The publishers of *The Tablet* (www.thetablet.co.uk), for permission to use material from an article of mine, 'Wake up call', which they published on 4 August 2012.

Bloomsbury Publishing plc for permission to quote from my chapter, 'The Merciful Economy' in Alistair McFadyen and Marcel Sarot (eds.), *Forgiveness and Truth* (T&T Clark, 2001), pp. 99ff.

CAFOD for permission to use material in 'Trading in Debt', in Rebecca Dudley and Linda Jones (eds.), *Turn the Tables* (CAFOD, 2003), pp. 15–18.

I have also gained enormously from the stimulus provided through invitations to speak about the issues examined in this book, and I have gained more than I know from the conversation and questioning which those invitations enabled to happen. In particular, I was honoured to be asked to give two lectures in Westminster Abbey, excerpts of which are included here:

'Structures of Disdain', the Gore lecture of 2006, was given by me at the invitation of the Dean and Chapter; and

'Misestablishment', the Eric Symes Abbott Memorial Lecture of 2012, I delivered there and at Keble College, Oxford, at the invitation of the lecture Trustees. The texts of both can be found at www.westminster-abbey.org/.

But these formal permissions reflect just a small part of the conversations I have had over the years since the 2008 crisis ('the tip of the iceberg' would do justice to the proportion but not to the warmth and fellowship of those many discussions!) and I cannot begin to recall by name all those who have encouraged me to pursue the issues and enriched me by their insights. However, the particular slant of this book, its reflections on and connection with idols and their worship, is one for which I need to take responsibility, and since I am still a member of the St Paul's Institute team I must make clear that the opinions expressed in this book are my own and not to be regarded as in any sense those of the Institute.

Jan, my wife, has now collected a number of experiences of what it is like to live with me while I am trying to write a book, and the gestation of this one, as well as the background activities associated with involvement in events to do with faith and economics, have continued to cause her to raise questions about what 'retirement' might ever mean in my case. It has certainly meant her giving me huge support and understanding during the process; without that this book would not have come to fruition, and for that I am far more grateful than I can say.

It gives me enormous pleasure to dedicate this book to my two most significant mentors and teachers. They have never met each other, but among many things they have in common their intellectual roots lie in the study of the Old Testament; although I have no pretensions to scholarship in that field of study, it will be evident from this book that their presentations of it left an indelible mark on my approach to faith. Neither of them is responsible for inaccuracies that may be apparent in my exegesis, but both of them gave me huge inspiration.

I was in my mid-teens when John Baker, then lecturing in Old Testament at King's College, London, came to live in our parish and was a regular preacher there. I learned from him that there was nothing more rewarding to think seriously about than Christian faith, and that that faith deserved language of the beauty and directness of which his sermons were such fine examples. Those qualities are evident in his well-known writings; he is also an example to me of the requirement that we follow our arguments to the point where, however inconvenient, they lead to truthful conclusions: whether on nuclear weapons, or on the ordination of women, or on human sexuality, he is well known for refusing to shy away from the conclusions of the Christian argument. When I came to serve as a bishop, John, then Bishop of Salisbury, was never far from my mind, representing so clearly that while bishops can avoid following the Christian argument to an inconvenient conclusion they do not have to do that, and indeed their calling is not to. To have enjoyed so long a friendship with the person to whom I owe the beginnings of my own faith has been a great honour and enrichment. Sadly John died between my writing the book and its publication, and so did not see the text; but it was good to hear from him that he was happy that he should be one of those to whom the book is dedicated.

It was nearly a decade after I met John that Harvey Guthrie, then Professor of Old Testament, and in charge of admissions, welcomed me into the stimulating and challenging environment of the Episcopal Theological School in Cambridge, Massachusetts. My two years there as a seminarian were life-changing years for which I have always been enormously grateful, but without question Harvey was for me as for many of my fellow students a person who provided seminal interpretations both of ancient texts and of the often turbulent events through which we were living in those days. Making connections between faith and the 'public square' is both demanding and inevitably contested; what is certain is that if that is to be done in a way that opens up debate rather than shutting it down the teacher, preacher and minister needs to be deeply involved equally in both text and event as well as in the community of his hearers. That level of involvement led Harvey to a way of teaching and preaching that was immensely memorable for us all, and has been for me a paradigm for the theological enterprise. Again, it is an enormous blessing to have been able to enjoy his friendship for all the decades since.

I hope what is written here is the kind of contribution to the following of the Christian argument that honours what I have received from two people to whose leading in faith and thought I owe so much.

Peter Selby
London, Eastertide 2014

Introduction – life in a casino

Money exercises a spectral power that exceeds all merely human powers. Adapting itself to any desire, it also shapes desire. In the first place, the value of money is transcendent: it is a promise, taken on faith, and only realised to the extent that this faith is acted out in practice in exchange. One cannot hold the value of money in one's hand, even if one can use the value to pay for things.

Philip Goodchild[1]

There may be some fashionable semi-philosophical scepticism about the continuous self, but it reflects a culture ... marked by compulsive withdrawal into a world of symbols that can be endlessly exchanged and manipulated, symbols that have lost their anchorage in a genuinely representation-oriented and therefore critical and exploratory engagement with the environment. Not to labour the point this is manifestly part of the toxic fascination of playing games with virtual wealth that has threatened the economic viability of whole nations in recent years.

Rowan Williams[2]

They have neither knowledge nor understanding; they walk about in darkness; all the foundations of the earth are shaken.

Psalm 82:5[3]

For very few are to be found who are of good cheer, and who neither mourn nor complain if they have not Mammon. This [care and desire for money] sticks and clings to our nature, even to the grave.

Martin Luther[4]

'It could be you'

I decided to get to the post office early to avoid (as I thought) a Saturday morning queue to buy some stamps. To my horror, at five minutes before opening time, there was already a long queue. But not for stamps: I had failed to take into account the fact that Saturday was the day to buy a ticket for that evening's National Lottery draw, and that was what the queue was about.

The faces of those waiting for opening time contrasted dramatically with the invitation they were responding to. The invitation on the board at the head of the queue said, 'Play the lottery', over the well-known, downward-pointing, crossed fingers that are the National Lottery logo, often with the strap line, 'It could be you'. But the faces were definitely not playful, rather grim and bored. They reminded me of the faces I had once seen facing one-arm bandits in Las Vegas as money was being fed, as by a robot, into the coin slot on the machine. The cycle kept being repeated: the coin fed in, the pull on the lever, the lost stake, the next coin. Occasionally there was a win; in that case the coins were gathered up and fed in until they too were exhausted.

The prospective purchasers of the lottery tickets were not (at least not yet) reduced to such robotic behaviour, and lottery tickets lack the addictive quality of the one-arm bandit. Nonetheless the image of the faces in the queue has stayed with me. 'Play the lottery'? Not at all like any other 'playing' we are used to. No smile, no excitement, just waiting to buy the ticket.

Another book about money

This is a book about money, what it has become, what it does and what it represents in our lives. In the years since I wrote about debt and its religious meaning,[5] the literature about money has grown vastly, and the implications of the monetary and banking crisis of 2008 and all that has followed from it have been analysed by official commissions, economists, economic historians and many others. The bibliography in this book is but a tiny part of the massive literature that now exists. The 2008 crisis has made money a much more fashionable topic of exploration than it had been, and excellent books like Felix Martin's *Money: The Unauthorised Biography* and Niall Ferguson's very different *The Ascent of Money* show up very graphically the role money has played and the vicissitudes through which it has passed; while David Marquand explores the dramatic consequences of what has happened to money in his recently published *Mammon's Kingdom: An Essay on Britain, Now.*[6] As we learn more of what money is and how it functions, we see certain patterns emerging in the way it is regarded and what it is doing to our society. The quite widely held view that money is not in itself harmful, only the love of it or greed for it, is turning out to be out of date, a view one might have been able to entertain when money was largely notes and coins, an instrument of trade and exchange. But something has happened in the years since the Second World War, a process of change that has accelerated as the twentieth century drew to its close and then exploded in the banking crisis of 2008.

More specifically, this book belongs in the category of *theological* books about money. It proposes that alongside the important insights contained in what economists and historians can tell us about money there is a *faith* aspect to what money has become. That is, money will not be rightly understood if it is not also seen in the light of the experience of the people who have seen the meaning of their lives in terms of a covenant relationship with the God of Abraham, Isaac and Jacob, the God who is the Father of Jesus Christ. There is within the literature and history of that people a wisdom about money that deserves to be taken seriously, and has in particular revealed its value significantly in the aftermath of the recent crisis. Much of that wisdom is to be found in the Bible, but because (as the Bible itself acknowledges) the covenant people have frequently ignored their own wisdom and departed from the covenant that gave their lives meaning, the struggle with money has had to continue: vows of poverty, heroic choices of various ways of life that renounce wealth for the sake of others, have been many believers' strategies for dealing with an aspect of life that they knew had its power and its dangers, dangers which they also knew tempted religious institutions to follow the way of money rather than the way of the covenant. Other traditions of faith, notably Islam, have noticed those departures and stand as a recall to a way of dealing with money that is loyal to divine commands.

Money has of course been examined theologically before: many have sought to recall believers to the priority of concern for the poor and the risks of developments such as globalisation where these are not held in check by a vision for humanity living together in justice and peace. The bibliography at the end of this book shows just a sample of the impressive work that has been done in the service of the conviction that following the way of money can have disastrous consequences, for humanity as well as for the planet we share with other species. But this has not just been a matter of the writing of books: believers have often led in the campaigns for justice and development, for reducing the impact of carbon emissions, for the defence of the world's biodiversity; many have been quite explicit in their campaigning that if humankind was to survive, let alone flourish, the making of money and the short-term thinking to which that goal often gives rise had to give way to objectives that are in the long-term interests of the world. And in the fifty years since the Congregational Union of Scotland published *Money, a Christian View*, the First Report of its Christianity and Wealth Committee,[7] the Christian Council for Monetary Justice has maintained in collaboration with many partner groups a small, very persistent campaign for monetary reform, while St Paul's Institute, with which I am also associated, has this among a number of topics in which it seeks to be in dialogue with financial sector institutions in the City of London.[8]

There have been other very important reflections on money as a theological issue. Peter Dominy's *Decoding Mammon*[9] is a strong wake-up call to take seriously modern developments in the character of money, and in particular its outworking in the changing of the nature of our desires; Philip Goodchild builds up a serious case in his *Theology of Money* against what he describes as the 'masquerade of [money's] moral neutrality'.[10] Equally, in the chapter on Money in its 2003 report *Being Human*, the Doctrine Commission of the Church of England underlines the point that so far from being a neutral substance about which human beings are free to entertain good attitudes and avoid bad ones – summed up as the *love* of money – money is in fact something that has the love of it embedded within what it has become.[11]

I seek in this book to build on that theological inheritance and to gain inspiration from the often very courageous stands taken by those who have thought through and worked out appropriate responses to what they rightly discerned to be a major challenge to humankind generally and believers in particular. This book, however, as well as being part of that developing tradition, is written for a very particular reason. I shall seek to show that alongside the developments I have already mentioned money has acquired the characteristics that were associated with the religions that worshipped *idols*. The significance of that term, one that has been used colloquially in the modern celebrity world, needs to be examined closely, and the ways in which money's behaviour, and our behaviour with money, echo the characteristics of the polytheistic world of the idols must be brought into clear view.

I shall describe in subsequent chapters the effect of money in its most recent developments on aspects of life which we would hope it might not affect. That is principally due to the vast expansion in the amount of money in the banking systems of the world and the speed with which computer technology allows it to circulate. Such growth, I shall suggest, has the inevitable result that what is more becomes more influential: our lives are more and more dominated by money, even when we think we are not particularly interested in it. We can see its effect on the way sovereign rule is exercised, because money has moved from being itself a sovereign act, authorised by the sovereign – whether that sovereign is an absolute monarch or a government that exercises authority in a parliamentary democracy – to being increasingly a virtual reality, created by private institutions as debt. We shall see just how powerful money and the private institutions that create it for their own profit have become.

God and the gods: life as a gamble

I began this chapter with a paragraph of personal experience of many years ago, in the early days of the National Lottery. That experience, for all its distance, has provided an image that has stayed with me, and which will, as we shall see, express the fundamental purpose of this book. Years have passed since I observed that queue outside the Post Office; the number of weekly draws and scratch card offers has grown vastly, alongside many new opportunities to gamble. The 'super-casino' debate was a very heated one, and in the interim we have had casinos developing and a massive growth in online gaming. Meanwhile in such a competitive world the National and Euro Lottery prizes, especially in rollover weeks, are sums of money way beyond the wildest dreams people entertain in their everyday lives. The industry has grown massively since that first week when the holder of a losing ticket was seen on television tearing up the ticket and exclaiming, with evident anger, 'This whole thing is just a lottery!'

All this is very profitable for those who provide the gambling opportunities. Alongside the growth of this industry has emerged a whole science of grant application, and across the country are now thousands of plaques on the walls of churches and other restored buildings acknowledging Heritage Lottery Fund grants, not to mention public acknowledgments of the support given by the Fund on a large scale to events like the Olympic Games.

What is going on here, before our very eyes? Who buys the tickets, and what is the net result of this increasingly popular activity, now regarded as a well-established part of life? Certainly there is concern for those who become addicted to gambling, and expressions of that concern in initiatives to help those who become trapped in that way. But what does this activity do to us as a society, and what does it represent?

My intention here is not to mount a conventional, puritanical attack on people enjoying themselves in some harmless pursuit. A congregation ending its harvest supper by raffling items that have been given to raise money is not, in my judgement, transgressing against the claims of the gospel. But the expansion of gambling into an industry of massive proportions is a very different matter. We know now that the original promise that nothing would be funded from the proceeds of the National Lottery that should be provided at a cost to the public purse was a false promise: it may indeed be that basic public services are not (so far) funded from lottery proceeds. But we also know that for any important task that is not currently part of what is provided from taxation, perhaps the necessary restoration of an ancient building or the construction of a new theatre or a local project to enable unemployed young people to find their way back into work or a new piece of medical equipment for the local hospital or most conspicuously the London Olympic Games, the first recourse will be to lottery funding.

We know other things too about this industry. We know that it tends to be the poorest who purchase the tickets. That is not because they are unwise in the handling of their limited money but on the entirely rational basis that for a person who sees no way out of their poverty even a very tiny chance of a win represents the most obvious way of solving their problem; by contrast, a person who already has sufficient money will know that there are far better ways of gaining more money than buying a lottery ticket.

As my initial story made clear, this is not in any normal sense of the word 'playing'; there is nothing playful about it. I am suggesting rather that once gambling becomes an industry and a major source of funding for public works it represents a belief system. I shall further suggest that that belief system is far from limited to those who 'play' it: the expansion in the role of money has co-opted humankind into values and practices which are at the heart of our monetary system and of which the events of 2008 were a sign and portent. We were brought to the edge of chaos when the lottery we are all playing produced not prizes but a disaster we need to learn from. To do that requires that we recover a very important piece of our ancient inherited wisdom. It is wisdom about what happens when you submit yourself to an idol. Others have mounted vital critiques of our monetary system, and what they have discovered we all need to take seriously. But there is a theological critique that needs to be mounted as well.

At the heart of the religious tradition of which we are the heirs is the story of an emerging conviction that life is not a gamble. The belief that it is one was widespread and very tempting, and we see that it still is. Because suffering is often inexplicable, it is very tempting to proclaim the view that all life is inexplicable too. For the ancients that view was often expressed in the form of myths that made the fate of human beings and nations the outcome of the capricious activities, conflicts and love affairs of divine beings. Those allegedly arbitrary roots of human history led to equally arbitrary attempts to win the lottery of life by processes of religious trial and error – so that, for instance, when animal sacrifice didn't seem to bring in the winning streak, it was natural to up the stakes and go for human sacrifice too.

Against this, our forbears in the faith took the enormous risk of trusting in – not gambling on – a God whose ways with the world were grounded in justice, morality and compassion, whose demands therefore were consistent with God's own character. Such a faith was hard to sustain, and was often forsaken in favour of a return to various forms of gambling on the roulette wheel of life. That was understandable; but it was also convenient for a more sinister reason: if people could be persuaded that life was *essentially* random in its outcomes or dependent on the activities of divine beings over whom they had no control they would be less likely to notice the contribution to their deprivation made by the anything but random machinations of those in power.

That is why debates about particular new gambling 'products' must not be allowed to pass in ignorance of what is at stake, and the churches' task is supremely to make that clear. We shall of course be told that people will and do gamble, and therefore we should provide for more of it and make money out of it for the needs of society. We shall also be told that nobody who engages in a parish raffle has any right to object, and that those who take money from the Heritage Lottery Fund have already decided for gambling and should not object to its expansion. But much more important for our purposes is that the link must be made not just to the events we know are gambling but to a financial system that represents a surrender to the notion that life itself is a lottery, in which massive winners must be allowed to keep their winnings while the losers endure their losses.

The fact is that when the National Lottery was debated warnings were uttered but not heeded; more importantly even the warnings failed to connect this development with the character of our monetary system itself: but we have lessons now that all can learn. The poorest are shown what the six numbered balls can offer them on a Saturday night, and so are persuaded to provide money of which a small proportion funds artistic enterprises and the restoration of churches. They then wake up on Sunday morning as poor as they were the day before, but having received the subliminal message that their poverty is the outcome simply of having picked the wrong numbers. That is light years removed from the small-stake, small-time raffles of small communities joining together for a bit of fun to produce some extra public good for their church or community. It is light years away because the two crossed fingers and the six numbered balls are now the symbols of a national belief system, one our ancestors rejected in the name of faith.

The ancient wisdom about idolatry requires that poverty and vulnerability are taken seriously precisely because their causes are not random, and their remedy does not lie in submission to a world where chance rules. Gambling addiction is not an accidental by-product of a glitzy fantasy in which Las Vegas is presented to the poorest members of society as the promised land; it is rather an added burden loaded on the shoulders of the poor by those not willing to make the modest social and fiscal sacrifices that would yield public good for all, and especially for the most needy. It is no coincidence that we have seen in recent years an international competition to remove the progressive elements in taxation, which have been the fairest way to care for the needy.

Money unmasked and an idol revealed

As the argument of this book proceeds it will become clear what money has become and what the world's current monetary system is doing. It is not, as will appear, an accident or the result of aberrant behaviour by a few greedy individuals – though there are many well-publicised examples of those who have profited to an obscene extent from a system that they would doubtless vigorously defend. What is important is to notice just how pervasive are the inroads the monetary system has made into institutions we have been taught we could trust and values by which we thought we were living. The way money is now created and manipulated, as I shall show, undermines democracy and the system of justice; it promotes inequality among individuals and nations, making the poor poorer even as it spectacularly enriches the wealthy. Because of its unrestricted global flows it limits the power of governments within their own borders. Because of the stimulus money in its vastly increased quantities and volatility provides to increasing consumption it has led to serious depletion of the planet's resources and unsustainable increases in carbon emissions.

That global effect is also reflected in the interior life of the human spirit. The prominence money has in our lives creates a climate of fear as the contrast appears ever greater between the rich and the poor – and therefore the possible fates that await us if we become poor. Pensions, the care of the elderly, the need for couples to have two incomes, the problems facing those seeking to buy their first home, the indebtedness of those who graduate, the postponement of marriage and child-bearing – all these and many other changes in individuals' and families' patterns of life are traceable to a system of money production that is in its most important respects unregulated, and constitutes for us all a personal and social burden of indebtedness. And worst of all, as has been indicated by the way this introduction began, it submits humankind to a situation which is always on the edge of chaos, always arbitrary and unpredictable in its outcomes, in short to life in a casino where the illusion offered by the few winners obscures the danger we are all in.

As the argument of the book proceeds it will be up against a major obstacle: the conviction that money is something we have to use and manage, that there is no other way of conducting our lives, and therefore contemplating the negative consequences of what money has become induces discomfort without offering any possibility of real change. Such is the nature of an idol: to maintain a hold on the mind so as to give the impression that it is natural, the only way things can be. As we cannot do without all that money can buy we are driven to assume that without what money has now become we cannot live.

It is a sobering reflection to notice that a similar idea prevailed two centuries ago in relation to slavery. As the poet William Cowper puts it with biting irony:

> I own I am shocked by the purchase of slaves
> And fear those who buy them and sell them are knaves.
> What I hear of their hardships, their torture, their groans
> Is almost enough to draw pity from stones.
> I pity them greatly, but I must be mum,
> For how could we do without sugar and rum?[12]

As we know with the benefit of hindsight, the discovery of alternative political and economic systems depended on courageous people declaring their conviction that slavery was *in principle* unacceptable, and therefore no amount of economic benefit for those who profited from the slave trade, or for the society of which they were a part, could justify the maintenance of that system. The statement that there is no economic alternative to our money-driven version of capitalism depends on categorising the attendant problems to which it is giving rise as merely *disadvantages* – therefore to be weighed according to a basically utilitarian calculus against other *advantages* – rather than outcomes which are fundamentally unacceptable. To look back at the process that led to the passage of legislation against the slave trade (we are all aware, of course, that there are still events that make reference to the 'ending' of the slave trade seem rather optimistic) is to be forced to register the ways in which economic arguments against ending it might have appeared plausible at the time; nobody could build a case for slavery on such arguments today. Once it was accepted that slavery was unacceptable, an alternative, and a strategy for achieving it, could be imagined. But first there had to be recognition that there was one compelling alternative to a trade in slaves, and that was not to have one.

Might it become true that a few generations from now the same position might seem the natural one to take about capitalism as it has now become? Is the increased prosperity of the rising middle class, traceable as it is to the 'achievements' of capitalism, something that can be said to 'outweigh' consequences which we can observe even now, let alone the ones that are part of the dangerous future that is coming towards us? Are these to be regarded as 'disadvantages' – as the exploitation and violation of persons that were intrinsic to slavery were once regarded? What might it take for generations to come to make a similar judgement about our present monetary system to the one we now make about slavery – that the negative consequences are not simply disadvantages but morally intolerable? When the list of capitalism's achievements is recited, will it seem reasonable to weigh these against the evidence of the destructive depletion of the planet's resources? Or against the production of excess greenhouse gases with the changes to the climate that follow from it? Is it not rather the case that these consequences flow inexorably from patterns of societal organisation and behaviour which are not changed largely because it would be unprofitable to some very powerful vested interests to change them? Do the well-documented consequences of unequal wealth distribution and the resulting plight of 'debtor' nations – the drug trade, the wars over resources, the proliferation of weapons traded for profit – appear to us as admittedly regrettable *disadvantages* of a capitalist system that is *necessary* for the general human prosperity? Are they what we tell ourselves we have to endure because we cannot imagine life without all the many equivalents of the sugar and rum that Cowper sarcastically declared to be the absolutely necessary requirements that justified the trade in slaves?

This book will look at what money has become and the consequences of that development, and seek to make the case that the consequences are so pervasive and so unacceptable that this has, first of all, to be owned, as idols have first of all to be named. Then, and only then, will the human mind be freed to discover the ways of reining money in, of dethroning this deity, and of the awakening of the imagination to the possibilities of so organising our economy that the human valuing transcends monetary valuing, that justice rather than consumption can become the overarching principle of human living. Till money is unmasked as the false deity, the idol that it is, we shall continue to be persuaded that money has to be in charge and money has to be the way it is. In Pope Francis' words:

> We have created new idols. The worship of the ancient golden calf (cf. *Ex* 32:1–35) has returned in a new and ruthless guise in the idolatry of money and the dictatorship of an impersonal economy lacking a truly human purpose. The worldwide crisis affecting finance and the economy lays bare their imbalances and, above all, their lack of real concern for human beings; man is reduced to one of his needs alone: consumption.[13]

Notes

[1] Philip Goodchild, *Theology of Money* (SCM Press, 2008), p. 12.

[2] Rowan Williams, from his Gifford Lectures, University of Edinburgh 2013.

[3] Psalm 82.5. Harvey Guthrie's observation of the sharp contrast between God and the gods in Psalm 82 have played a very large part in my reflections on idolatry.

[4] Martin Luther, 'The First Commandment' in *Large Catechism* (1580). See Theodore G. Tappert (ed.), *The Book of Concord* (Fortress Press, 1959), p. 360.

[5] See my *Grace and Mortgage* (Darton, Longman & Todd, 1997, reissued 2009).

[6] Felix Martin, *Money: The Unauthorised Biography* (Bodley Head, 2014); Niall Ferguson, *The Ascent of Money: A Financial History of the World* (Allen Lane, 2008); David Marquand, *Mammon's Kingdom: An Essay on Britain, Now* (Allen Lane, 2014).

[7] George F. McLeod, *Money: A Christian View. First Report of the Christian Doctrine of Wealth Committee* (Congregational Union of Scotland, 1963).

[8] Christian Council for Monetary Justice, www.ccmj.org; St Paul's Institute, www.stpaulsinstitute.org.uk.

[9]   Peter Dominy, *Decoding Mammon* (Wipf and Stock, 2012), see especially pp. 86–99.

[10] Philip Goodchild, *Theology of Money* (SCM Press, 2008), p. 181.

[11] Doctrine Commission of the Church of England, *Being Human* (Church House Publishing, 2003), pp. 55–77.

[12] William Cowper, 'Pity for Poor Africans' in William Cowper, *The Poetical Works of William Cowper* (William P. Nimmo, 1863), pp. 418f.

[13] Pope Francis, *Evangelii Gaudium* (Vatican Press, 2013), para. 55.

2

Whatever happened to our money?

Then the Pharisees went and plotted to entrap him in what he said. So they sent their disciples to him, along with the Herodians, saying, 'Teacher, we know that you are sincere, and teach the way of God in accordance with truth, and show deference to no one; for you do not regard people with partiality. Tell us, then, what you think. Is it lawful to pay[1] taxes to the emperor, or not?' But Jesus, aware of their malice, said, 'Why are you putting me to the test, you hypocrites? Show me the coin used for the tax.' And they brought him a denarius. Then he said to them, 'Whose head is this, and whose title?' They answered, 'The emperor's.' Then he said to them, 'Give[2] therefore to the emperor the things that are the emperor's, and to God the things that are God's.' When they heard this, they were amazed; and they left him and went away.

(Matthew 22.15–22)

Without doubt something has been happening to our money. For sure, we have seen events over the last decade that have given us all a shock. The queues seeking to withdraw their money from Northern Rock were of people who reckoned there was a good chance that they would lose their money. Food banks have multiplied, as a significant section of our society has found that the money they had relied on – not just those in receipt of welfare benefits but those on relatively low wages – now lacked the power to enable their payment of rent and provision of food. Governments have had to

An Idol Unmasked

take steps that they would previously never have contemplated: the nationalising of banks for fear they were about to fail; the reduction of interest rates to very near to nil for fear the economy would grind to a halt; guaranteeing loans to people to buy houses for fear the 'housing market' would cease to function. At the same time a programme of cuts in welfare expenditure which far exceeds any undertaken in the past is running its course.

These are some of the marks of what is generally regarded as a global economic crisis, dating in most accounts from the collapse in August 2008 of Lehman Brothers, a previously unthinkable insolvency in both scale and suddenness. They are what comes into most people's minds when they hear talk about an economic crisis. There was very little debate about whether governments worldwide had to intervene dramatically to prevent a serious crisis turning into a total collapse, with devastating consequences for the ordinary and necessary activities of trade and the sustaining of daily life. There continues to be much more debate about who was to blame for the crisis in the first place, and who should be held to account for the enormous public debt involved in the bailouts and rescues that governments have felt obliged to undertake.

If catastrophe was warded off, grave consequences for very vulnerable people and communities were not. Many of the measures that were presented as necessitated by the crisis were also – or, some would certainly say, principally – opportunities for implementing changes ('reforms') that were long-standing political ambitions: changing allowances for jobseekers, altering the criteria for receiving disability benefits, tightening the rules governing welfare payments to immigrants among others. As controversial are questions about whether the changes are 'working', whether the more 'encouraging' growth figures are evidence of real economic recovery, and whether that recovery is sustainable over the longer term, and firmly enough established to give confidence that the crisis is, or is on the way to being, over.

All the signs are that whatever may be the view that triumphs in that argument – that the recovery is established or that it is not – the policies that will be pursued will be more of the same: if the economy's recovery is deemed not to be fully established, then further measures to 'finish the job' will be implemented; if it is deemed not to be recovering then the argument will be that even tougher measures will be required to do that. Thus the ideological roots of what pass as economic debates become ever clearer, and despite all the research that reveals that higher levels of inequality produce stresses and strains on individuals and society at large, the view that governs policy is the opposite. Those who are wealthy are said to require even larger rewards to encourage them to exercise their expertise; those who are poor are said to be in need of negative incentives to encourage them to work harder. Thus the pressures are all to widen further the gaps that are already wider than at any time in history. Not surprisingly, Richard Wilkinson and Kate Pickett, in their famous *The Spirit Level*, sense themselves both to accord with a deep-seated awareness in many that greater equality leads to greater social happiness and at the same time to be swimming against the tide of much contemporary post-crisis political posturing. But they are very determined in saying what needs to happen:

> It is now time egalitarians returned to the public arena. We need to do so confident that our intuitions have been validated and found to be truer than most of us ever imagined.[3]

Yet it is the contrary direction – towards increased inequality – that continues to dominate our political processes and, if public opinion polls are anything to go by, that direction commands widespread support even from people who in supporting it are in effect voting against themselves. We shall have cause to return later to the effect of the crisis and its aftermath on the character of our democracy. Part of the reason for the level of support for actions that disadvantage further those who are already the most disadvantaged is a failure to understand at sufficient depth the roots of the crisis through which we are passing. The fact is that its roots lie precisely in the very ideas and activities which are so taken for granted that any threat to them is seen as a threat to everyone. So despite the level of imprudence that lay behind the crisis of 2008, examples abound of corporate decisions which must be based on a belief that those who gained most rewards before the crisis need to continue to be amply rewarded if they are to stay on hand to rescue our economy from the disaster for which they were largely responsible. There appears to be a surprising failure to comprehend that there can be no improvement of the ethical climate of institutions that were dysfunctional without also addressing the enormous size of pay and bonuses.[4] What this fails to take into account is that money has become one of the largest factors in determining the ethical climate of institutions and of society at large.

To understand how it comes about that so many continue to support systems and supposed remedies which so evidently lay behind the 2008 crisis it is necessary to see what it is that has so embedded those attitudes in our consciousness to the extent that we hardly know they are there. For attitudes do not precede the behaviours that issue from them; rather, it is repeated behaviour, behaviour that starts by being apparently unavoidable, that embeds attitudes which then go on to support further manifestations of the same behaviour. So the attitude of students to being in debt has been completely changed by the creation of an environment in which being in debt is quite simply necessary, confirmed in later life by the fact that a mortgage is seen as the only acceptable way of purchasing a home.[5] Any negative attitude to being in debt has been superseded by a positive one, simply because borrowing is absolutely necessary for such basic aspirations as participating in higher education and obtaining a home.

What has to be examined therefore is our behaviour with money and the assumptions which lie behind it. It is what has happened to money, and what are the behaviours with money that are now assumed to be necessary, that create a whole range of social attitudes, political creeds and even religious beliefs that in turn entrench those behaviours and establish them as the basis of society. To know why it is that we think as we do about money we need to begin with an examination of what it is that has happened to our money under our very noses. We shall need in fact to ask ourselves the uncomfortable question, is it 'our' money at all: do we own the money, or has money come to own us?

Money: a long history speeds up

> It does not mean that the pound here in Britain, in your
> pocket or purse or in your bank, has been devalued.[6]

When Harold Wilson, then Prime Minister, addressed the nation
following his government's decision to devalue sterling he made
good rhetorical use of what it is our instinct to think money is. It
is what you have in your pocket, your purse, your bank account.
It is a reliable unit of value, something we can trust. The sense of
that reliability is confirmed when we hold a pound coin, its colour
– though not its content – reminiscent of the gold sovereign. It
has weight and durability, and we want to believe our money has
both those qualities as well. And even when it is 'paper money'
we expect it to have an intricate pictorial design, the sovereign's
picture, the signature of the Chief Cashier of the Bank of England,
promising to pay the bearer the amount denoted on the piece of
paper. The paper may not be worth much, but behind it lies, we
like to think, whatever the mysterious modern equivalent might be
of the bullion in the vaults of the Bank of England, the source of
ultimate durability and reliability, the guarantee that our money is
sound. So Harold Wilson thought he could reassure the electorate
about the value of the pound in their pocket without their noticing
that devaluation would lead to inflation.

The obverse of that belief in the reliability of money is the
sense that the greatest failure of government – apart from not
defending the safety of the realm – is to pursue policies that shatter
the illusion that money is possessed of permanence and reliability.
It did not take long for Wilson's political opponents to point out
that this rhetorical appeal was to an illusion: the pound would now
buy fewer dollars, and as a result exports would be cheaper for
overseas buyers and imports dearer for those who had to buy them
in the shops with the 'pound in their pocket'. The unchanging had
changed. Devaluation is not the only way in which a government
can undermine that sense of permanent value: the hyperinflation
which afflicted the Weimar republic in the 1920s is etched into

German folk memory and strengthens their resolve that inflation is to be avoided at all – or nearly all – costs. From the other side of the British political battle, Margaret Thatcher famously cut a 'Labour pound' in two to illustrate the inflation over which Labour had presided: money can lose its durability and reliability – but it is up to government to make sure it does not do so.

That is not of course what governments actually do. Governments – all governments – use money, manipulate the value of money, use the power of taxation to alter its distribution and regulate its uses, all to further their chosen political ends or their chosen response to events. So when – to quote a current example from this wettest of winters – the Prime Minister visits the Somerset Levels in order to demonstrate his sympathy for residents and farmers overwhelmed by floods, he can say that 'whatever money is needed will be spent'; and because of the enormity of the suffering the inhabitants are enduring nobody will be so churlish as to point out that such a statement is completely at variance with the oft-repeated policy of the government that the ending of its budget deficit is its top priority. When the money is needed – in terms of political priority – it is there. Not only does nobody point out the inconsistency of allowing what in other contexts would be called profligacy – perhaps even 'tax and spend' – nobody even dares to ask what other expenditure will be sacrificed to make this particular priority possible.

So the 'pound in your pocket' is a rather more malleable entity than the hard golden-looking coins or the impressively watermarked and decorated notes would suggest or our deeply cherished illusions about money would require. In his elegant and highly readable history of money,[7] Felix Martin leaves in pieces most of what we have cherished about the character of money, that it has the fixity of an 'object', and that it emerged in order to be a more convenient way of trading than barter would have been. He points out with copious illustrations that there never were 'objects' of fixed worth that could be exchanged for any number of things that people might need. Money did not emerge, as we often suppose, because butchers had surplus meat but had as much bread or beer as they needed and so had no use for the only things the local baker or brewer might be able to supply in exchange for the meat they wanted to obtain.[8] Rather, money emerged from the willingness of people to place their trust in one of the many items that have served as money down the generations. And what enabled them to place their trust in an item so as to allow it to serve as money was the knowledge that someone else would accept it as such. Money is credit because people were willing to 'credit' it, to believe that it would serve its purpose as a means of trade and exchange.

This does not of course mean that the mechanisms by which governments establish a currency and regulate it, produce coins and notes and attest them, are irrelevant, or that when it comes to serving as money 'anything will do'. There is a reality to the power of sovereign authority to validate certain objects as money, to declare what it will accept as government, for instance for the payment of taxes. I can sign an IOU, and there is nothing to stop a person accepting it, and then if they choose passing it to someone else in payment for some goods or services; but the reality is that they are far more likely to accept it if it is denominated in units which the sovereign authority has recognised and, ultimately, will back as 'legal tender'. It is because of its power to control resources that the sovereign authority is uniquely credited with the power to create and validate 'real money'; that in turn is the reason why the money that is created and validated by the sovereign establishes in the minds of citizens that money is an object endowed with permanence and reliability. But if that is generally so, we should be aware that there are numerous historical examples of states whose citizenry have for various reasons lost confidence in the money the sovereign has validated – in times of hyperinflation, for instance – and have generated their own forms of credit and 'money' because they were able to repose more trust in those forms of money than in the ones generated by the state. This is simply to make the point that money exists where and in so far as people believe in it. Generally they will believe in the state's money, but it is the belief and not the fact of state validation – of legal tender – that makes money fit for purpose as money.

That brings us to the discussion between Jesus and his Pharisee interlocutors about paying taxes to Caesar, the discussion quoted at the start of this chapter. Jesus asks them to produce a coin not simply for a pedagogical purpose: by pointing to a coin and to the fact of the Pharisees' possession of it he establishes that if behind the question of paying taxes to Caesar lies some religious point of view that handling tainted, Gentile, currency makes them unclean, or a political sense that the taxes were supporting the occupying power, then in order to be consistent they ought not to allow themselves to hold or possess such money. That they were able to produce a coin validated by Caesar's image and name indicated that they were perfectly prepared to engage in commerce or trade using his currency. Jesus drives his point home by altering the verb in the Pharisees' question: they ask 'Is it lawful to *pay* (*dounai*) tribute to Caesar', implying that in paying tribute they were parting with what was theirs; he answers, '*Give back* (*apodote*) to Caesar what is Caesar's', for by possessing Caesar's currency they had already answered their own question: they were part of his system, recognising his sovereignty, so that paying the appropriate amount to him was no more than *giving back* to him what was already his in any case. They were part of Caesar's economy with the advantages and responsibilities that flowed from it; that was a decision they had made. The concluding, sharp, comment is the assertion that in the same way they were also part of God's economy, and were to restore to God what was God's; what they thought of as their sacrificial offerings were already God's.

As well as the moral and theological point that this story makes, it reveals something very significant about the journey money has taken in modern times. Here we have in the New Testament a story that illustrates that in effect money, that to which people could credit the power to be money, was subject to the sovereign's creation, validation and regulation. Nobody would be allowed to create their own kind of money any more than they would be allowed to create their own kind of army. Money had to have Caesar's writ behind it or its value could not be relied on. And whatever might have been the theoretical and sometimes actual possibilities of passing credit from one to another the overwhelming power of the creation and regulation of money was an aspect of sovereignty.

The outward appearances of that world have remained: coins bear the sovereign's image and inscription; notes bear the sovereign's image and the promise of the central bank to validate a monetary note as money. But as we shall see, decisions which were taken during the last century set in train a course of events which have made money into a very different kind of commodity. In particular, as we shall consider in more detail in the next chapter, the sovereign's actual authority over money has come to be shared with all sorts of other agencies and corporations. The developments of recent decades amount to a huge transfer of sovereign power, and there is no sign that it is likely to be reversed.

Quantity and volatility

It might seem on the face of it sensible enough for banks, provided they keep an adequate reserve, to lend to others a multiple of what has been deposited with them; after all, most of the time it seems safe to assume that not all customers are going to want access to their money at the same time. The system has continued through centuries, interrupted by occasional crises but generally well enough respected. But it is easy enough for the system – fractional reserve banking – to move from one that allows banks to lend money to others and only keep a fraction of their assets in reserve to one in which banks can, and do, lend large multiples of the deposits they hold. What this means in practice is that the overwhelming majority of the money banks lend is debt, money created out of nothing by the activity of lending what the bank does not have but instead borrows. Nobody is surprised to learn that banks charge more for the money they lend than what they pay to their depositors – therein lies their profit. But what is carefully glossed over, so as not to enter the consciousness of the public, is that most of the money the banks lend so profitably is not theirs or their depositors', but is simply created out of thin air. The profit is not the interest earned from borrowers minus the interest paid to lenders: it is to a massive extent the interest they receive on money they have created.

What is more, this change from money as validated by the sovereign to a system where money is simply created by banks does not lead only to the financing of economically useful products and activities, but has generated a vast and complicated market in money itself, changing it from what facilitates trade and exchange to an object of speculation in itself. Loans of money are bought and sold, packaged as 'financial products', on the basis that the originator hopes that his or her 'product' will increase in value. This 'money' is not enabling productive economic activity but in effect simply creating more of itself.

But such a system, however well it might appear to operate in gentle times, is highly vulnerable, and has proved to be so in recent decades as a result of two significant developments: massive increases in the quantity of money finding its way into the banking system as a result (principally) of the oil price rises in the later decades of the twentieth century, alongside the technological changes made possible by computerisation. Money has, as a result, increased vastly in quantity and in the speed with which it can be circulated. The speed multiplies the effect of the increased quantity, and both are multiplied as a result of financial institutions' ability to lend multiples of the money they hold as deposits.

The result has been a feverish expansion in debt, reflected in lending to countries of the two-thirds world on the one hand and in housing and consumer indebtedness on the other.[9] The fever came down to one thing: the need of banks to make sure that the vastly increased supply of money they had to lend, and the even greater amount they were able to create, made profits for them. The ancient Greeks called interest *tokos*, offspring: interest is the ability of money to clone itself, and that ability has grown by leaps and bounds. The result is a world in which the best way to make money is to have money, and the more the better. So there has emerged a huge diversion of the ingenuity of the corporate executives of institutions whose overriding aim is to be profitable, from making things and offering services to working out new and cleverer ways of making money out of money. It is widely recognised that the crisis of 2008 was in large measure the result of the grotesquely imprudent exercise of that ingenuity, with the result that the trade in money became more and more distant from the real economic activity – making things or providing services – which is what money is actually for. As Bishop David Jenkins once famously described it, it became to a huge extent a matter of 'people making money out of people making money out of people making money out of people making what?'[10]

Of course, such high levels of lending and speculation have generated real economic activity and inventiveness along the way. The world continues to be transformed by new products, new ways of working, new forms of leisure activity. The point is not that *all* of the huge flows of money are without effect in the real economy; however, the over-heating which has resulted diverted the abilities of too many people and institutions into activities which were only justified by the fact that they made money out of the manipulation of money.

As when the quantity of water generates pressures which rivers and lakes cannot contain and dams cannot hold back, this explosion in the quantity of money and the speed of its circulation burst the dams of the restraints and regulation which had been part of the financial scene. The 'big bang', the transformation on 27 October 1986 of much of the regulation that had governed the London Stock Exchange, was a highly symbolic event, a response to the irresistible pressure of money transactions and the computerisation of share dealings. It was part of a decade of 'liberalisation' which was at once technical – through the computerisation of finance – and ideological.

More than one kind of restraint proved casualty to this decade in which the prevailing political view was that there was no alternative to a revolutionary change in response to the amount and the speed with which money transactions could now be carried out. All forms of resistance, whether in the name of workers' rights or the priority of maintaining a strong manufacturing sector, were seen as an essentially Luddite response which, if pursued, would lead to impoverishment and stagnation. The victory of this way of thinking was well-nigh complete as an international consensus developed that there was only one way to go.

If political restraints gave way to the pressure of money's quantity and volatility, so inevitably did significant ethical restraints also. The events of 2008 have set in train investigations, likely to be ongoing for the foreseeable future, into activities by high-flying traders, many of whom appear to have gained vastly excessive rewards for financial ingenuity rather than ingenuity of more socially useful kinds; well-publicised cases where that lack of restraint and the temptation of huge financial rewards led to notorious and criminal behaviour are still in the headlines, and will remain there for some time to come. Some individuals may be more prone to addictive greed than others; but it is not at all surprising to find that a system in which money is given such priority leads people to throw aside necessary inhibitions. We are on a very fast-moving train.

Much of the argument that will occupy later chapters has to do with what happens when a substance such as money acquires the pre-eminence that it has acquired in recent decades. The existence of the love of money is as old as money itself, and there have always been those led into wrongdoing as a result. But what has happened to money in recent decades is that its trajectory and speed of growth in the economy has been reflected in a similar growth in the place it occupies in our consciousness. We are on a journey, it seems, in which money moves from being an invention that allows human beings to engage in constructive exchange to being a key aim in itself. With that comes the reality that what is an end in itself becomes the guiding political and ethical principle; the sovereign is no longer the name of a coin, generated by sovereign authority. Money becomes itself the sovereign guide to legislative and ethical conviction. And as we shall see as this argument proceeds, with the arrival of such a conviction comes, as night follows day, the time when money is a deity, an idol to be worshipped.

Notes

1 Gk. *dounai*, to give or pay.
2 Gk. *apodote*, give back.

3   Richard Wilkinson and Kate Pickett, *The Spirit Level* (Penguin, 2010), p. 298.

4   For a fuller discussion of the attempt to reform a corporate ethical climate without addressing the issue of bonuses, see below pp. 120 – 122.

5   See my discussion of student debt in *Grace and Mortgage* (Darton, Longman & Todd, 1997, 2009), pp. 46ff. and housing debt, *ibid.*, pp. 35ff.

6   Harold Wilson, broadcasting to the nation on 19 November 1967. See http://news.bbc.co.uk/onthisday/hi/dates/stories/november/19/newsid _3208000/3208396.stm.

7   Felix Martin, *Money: The Unauthorised Biography* (The Bodley Head, 2013).

8   Martin quotes Adam Smith's illustration in 'Of the Origin and Use of Money', as showing that even this great figure of the history of economics held the view that money is thus a replacement of barter. See Martin, *Money*, p. 7. For a detailed account of how money is created in the banking system, see a recent Bank of England Quarterly Bulletin article, Michael McLeay, Amar Radia and Ryland Thomas, 'Money Creation in the Modern Economy' (www.bankofengland.co.uk/publications/Documents/ quarterlybulletin/2014/qb14q102.pdf).

9   Both these developments are described in much more detail in my *Grace and Mortgage*, pp. 30–58, 73–93.

10 This one-liner is more fully developed in his *Market Whys and Human Wherefores* (Cassell, 2000).

3

When money rules

In recent years, no large Western democracy has been more
devoted to money worship than Britain. It helped to spawn
the heady boom of the early noughties; it drove the growth of
inequality that has been a prime feature of British society for
nearly thirty years; and it has survived the bust that began with
the run on Northern Rock in 2008. Yet, in all the anguished
debates that have followed, the deeper issues involved have
rarely been discussed.

David Marquand [1]

What this vast quantitative change has actually brought about
is a great qualitative change – money is no longer a servant,
but a master.

Peter Dominy [2]

Money and power

As we have seen, money has grown and grown – that much is
clear. It has grown vastly in quantity: fractional reserve banking
means in effect 'multiple lending banking' – banks lend a large
multiple of what has been deposited with them; the vast influx of
money into the banking system in the last quarter of the twentieth
century, particularly since the major oil price rises of the 1970s,
caused a massive change in the national and world economy,
enormously accentuated by banks' practice of lending multiples of
their deposits. Add to that the technology that allows money to

circulate in microseconds, and the world has experienced a huge increase in the weight that money carries. The idea that money has always been a source of temptation and that therefore there is nothing new in our current attachment to it leaves out of account these massive changes. Power has accumulated alongside money, and the power that has accumulated is such that where money used to carry the sovereign's authority, and that was the source of the trust that could be placed in it, we have moved to a situation where money has taken on much of the role of sovereign, directing and authorising the exercising of power in society at large, nationally and internationally. The head and the name of the sovereign still appear on coins and notes; the central bank inscribes notes with a guarantee of their continued legal tender; but the reality is that money has long since passed from the control of public authorities, and has become itself the major controlling force behind the organisation of society. Money may continue to be used as though nothing has happened; but even as we apparently carry on with business as usual, power is being exercised by what we would still like to think is under our control. If we think that, we are deluding ourselves.

The power of money, therefore, to direct our lives needs further analysis. For that power is not just power in a general sense of influence or pressure: it is increasingly *sovereign* power, and sovereign power is power of a particular quality. We are aware that the way in which sovereign power has been exercised has passed through numerous changes in the course of history: sovereignty used to be exercised by an absolute monarch; during the last century many of the absolute monarchies, particularly those in Europe, have mutated into constitutional monarchies, exercised on the advice of governments who are elected by various forms of popular suffrage; arguably they have only survived as titular monarchies because of their willingness to embrace that change, with whatever degree of reluctance. Such are changes in the way in which sovereign power is exercised: monarchies that have survived have done so by and large as a result of accepting that process, allowing the delegation of their powers to elected officials. However the character of that power as *sovereign* is what needs to be considered; the fact that power is acquired by means of a popular mandate does not alter the fact that *sovereign* power has a very particular force.

What distinguishes *sovereign* power is that it is the ultimate power in human affairs: it has what has been traditionally been designated *vitae necisque potestas*, the 'power of life and death'. Giorgio Agamben also argues that in the modern state, sovereign power has become power over people's capacity to survive day by day: it is power over *bare life*.[3] This is hardly an abstract point of constitutional theory: it is not difficult to find graphic illustrations of the way in which sovereign power, even when it does not have the capacity to order the deaths of individuals for wrongdoing, nonetheless increasingly determines the capacity of large numbers of people to house themselves and their families, to feed themselves, to be treated in the event of bodily illness, to find basic education for their children, or to obtain productive employment; for all citizens of the state to some degree, and for the poorest citizens to an ever increasing degree, the state's 'power over bare life' continues to grow. Thus politics becomes *bio*politics, the politics that governs life itself; the sovereign has overwhelming power over basic, bodily, existence, and even when that power is not directly exercised its existence constitutes the basic promise or threat that overshadows the life of all citizens whether they are conscious of it or not.

The point needs to be stressed: the argument here is not affected by the *processes by which* sovereign power has been exercised. It would be a mistake to suppose that the character of sovereign power has changed simply because the *mechanisms* of constitutional government or democratic elections are in place; as we shall see, the opposite can be the case.

For while the sovereign is without question created and designated as part of the juridical order of the society, with rights and duties constitutionally prescribed, the sovereign also has the capacity to define the boundaries of the constitutional order; that is, the sovereign has the right to declare *status exceptionis*, a 'state of exception', the point at which the protections to which citizens are entitled have to give way before 'the security and well-being of the state': the debates about welfare provision all assume that it is the right of the sovereign (that is to say, the government) to determine whether the bare necessities of life will be available to a person who is unable for whatever reason to secure them for herself. It is of the essence of sovereignty that it is defined by its capacity to decide the exception, who, that is, and in what circumstances the citizen is excluded from the rights offered by the constitutional order, and when the sovereign authority can act outside its constraints. And it is the exception, as Kierkegaard puts it, that tells you what sovereign power is:

> The exception explains the general and itself. And when one really wants to study the general, one need only look around for a real exception. It brings everything to light more clearly than the general itself.[4]

Describing sovereignty in terms of the right to declare an exception points to the sovereign's right to declare the subject excluded from the society, in particular its protections and benefits. Sovereign power thus shows itself in things like the right to imprison, to section under the mental health acts, or to deprive of citizenship or residence.

It is unfortunately a fact of history that examples of the exercise of this sovereign power to exclude and ultimately to kill are not hard to find, and such examples are not just to be seen in the past. They demonstrate all too clearly that particular constitutional arrangements for the exercise of sovereign power are far from being a guarantee against the placing of individuals and groups under 'bans' of various kinds, sanctions which deprive them of what they need for bare life. What is important, however, is that the totalitarian regimes of the twentieth century are considered not simply as the singular extremisms of particular countries and times, but are seen in the context of the development of precisely those institutions that were thought to liberate people from the sovereign's uncontrolled power. In particular, it would be important not to see democracy, the 'sovereignty of the people', as some kind of guarantee against exceptional and extreme exercises of sovereign power.

In fact democratic institutions, based as they are on the belief that popular power will be the best defence of popular interests against the power of those who direct armies or have the control of most of the wealth, have proved easy prey to those able to engage the sympathies of the populace against vulnerable groups of many kinds. To engage the people it is only necessary to persuade them – or perhaps it might sometimes be more appropriate to say 'seduce' them – into believing that those with power and wealth are their best protection against groups who are for their part presented as the greatest danger to their prosperity or even their very safety. The politics of bare life, the increased ability of government to determine who shall and who shall not have the means of bare life, or who is to be regarded as the greatest danger to the security of the majority, can easily be manipulated into achieving a situation where sovereign power becomes even more secure and less subject to control. The sovereign is able to designate particular individuals and groups as presenting an enormous risk to the security of the state, or to the prosperity and well-being of 'the people', and therefore as not deserving the protections citizens are meant to enjoy. The paradox is that the greater the capacity of the state to provide for the needs of the people – for instance for security, health and education – the greater is the state's capacity to secure its place and its power, and therefore the greater is its immunity from that public accountability which democratic institutions were intended to secure.

There are echoes here of the ancient warnings about Hebrew kingship, a kingship created also in response to the 'will of the people', albeit expressed in a pre-modern society. The people are warned that the king will take their sons for his armies and their daughters as cooks, perfumers and bakers; the best of the produce of the land will be taken for his purposes. And then, in words that echo much of the history of 'chosen' sovereigns, 'you will cry out because of your king whom you have chosen for yourselves; but the LORD will not answer you in that day'. (1 Samuel 8.18)

So it was that the 'river of biopolitics', the progressive concern of sovereign power with bare life, came together with the plan of the twentieth-century totalitarian states for total domination, working itself out most terrifyingly in the concentration camps. As Hannah Arendt puts it:

> The concentration camps are the laboratories in the experiment of total domination, for human nature being what it is, this goal can be achieved only under the extreme circumstances of human-made hell.[5]

For those of us to whom 'concentration camps' are a phenomenon of the Third Reich, it is profoundly disturbing to note that 'concentration camps' were developed by the Spanish in their colonisation of Cuba at the end of the nineteenth century and by the British in their dealings with the Afrikaaners at the same time. In both cases, the needs of the colonists resulted in the declaration of a 'state of exception', effectively of martial law. By the time such a state of exception was declared within the Nazi state to provide the basis for the camps, it was not even necessary to make an open declaration of a 'state of exception' as such, so much had that extreme situation become part of the normal operation of the state.

In its courageous statement on war responsibility,[6] the Synod of the *Nippon Seiko-Kai*, the Japanese province of the Anglican Communion, makes a number of similar points about the rule of the *Tenno*, the Japanese Emperor. The Synod's statement points to the idolatry inherent in the *Tenno* system, seeing it as the root of the imperialism and racism, in which obedience to the 'God of Heaven' or 'King of the Universe' is validated by an interior obedience on the part of the subjects who identify their interests and their destiny with the power of the sovereign. The theme of idolatry is the central one of this book, and will be examined in more detail in the next two chapters; the point here is that money has come, because of the expansion of its role, its quantity and its ubiquity, to exercise much of the power previously associated with the sovereign.

In the traditions of sovereignty as exercised in English history idolatry of the sovereign is in a formal sense avoided. But that formal avoidance does not counter the point that sovereign power as exercised domestically and then exported is indeed sovereignty over bare life, and so all life. The prayer for the sovereign in the

Holy Communion service of the Book of Common Prayer is that 'she (knowing whose minister she is) may above all things seek thy honour and glory'. The formal idolatry is avoided by the clause 'knowing whose minister she is'; however, the balancing clause contains the more important assertion,

> and that we and all her subjects (duly considering whose authority she hath) may faithfully serve, honour and humbly obey her, in thee, and for thee, according to thy blessed word and ordinance.

The elegant rhetorical symmetry presented by these two clauses cannot conceal the serious and deliberate imbalance of substance. The prayer that worshippers offer for the sovereign is counterbalanced by the assertion of divine authority and scriptural backing for the total obedience of the subjects. It hardly needs adding that what is asked of the subjects is subject to enforcement, as those who belonged to different Christian allegiances or lands later colonised knew well when they found themselves experiencing the sovereign's rule over bare life.

Sadly, the 'river of biopolitics' flows on, as those dependent on the state for 'bare life' now endure the effect of changed policies for welfare and public provision: as one London landlord was reported to say, the evictions he needed to seek because of caps on housing benefit would amount in effect to 'ethnic cleansing'.[7] The disproportionate incarceration of members of poor and disadvantaged groups and minority ethnic communities witnesses to the same point. Both the welfare regime and the increased use of imprisonment show what sovereignty actually means, and provide the threatening context within which all who are citizens, whether wealthy or impoverished, powerful or marginalised, pass their lives. The fact that sovereign power is now based on a democratic mandate is not much protection for the most vulnerable if the populace has been persuaded to yield to the blandishments of the strong and to take sides against those in greatest need. And that persuasion has much to do with the movement towards the sovereign power of money, for the ubiquitous presence of advertising is geared not simply to inviting preferences for one product rather than another, but to commending a way of life that depends on impressing upon the populace just what it is that money can do for them – while the news shows many examples of its obverse, the threat of the desperate struggle for bare life among those who do not have that most significant necessity of life, namely money.

Democratic processes and the constitutional relationships that are its outward forms certainly give opportunities for exercising an effect on what government does, on legislation, on the institutions of civil society. To take those opportunities is perfectly proper, as it is to resist what is done in the name of citizens but fails the test of justice. However, over all of those activities is a warning sign that reads, 'Remember the power of the state, even if exercised in your name, to determine whether you will have the means of livelihood or not'; crisis, the point of judgement, comes when sovereign power, *vitae necisque potestas*, is actually exercised, where persons are made, economically or by the use of force, non-persons: at that point the decision is whether to side with sovereign power or with the victims of its use, whatever that decision might cost; for what is clear is that government decisions are overwhelmingly influenced by the way money has come to work in our time.

The effect of monetary growth is sometimes overt and sometimes extremely subtle, but equally significant in either case. Twelve fellow citizens are required to determine the guilt or innocence of an accused person; such is one of the most ancient protections of the liberty of the subject. But what happens if the outsourcing of the state's custody arrangements has reached the point where large public companies obtain contracts to run prisons? It is too easy to say that the twelve fellow citizens are not influenced by financial considerations, something that on the face of it is clearly true: criminal attempts to bribe jurors are fortunately rare. But jurors are also persons in a society increasingly concerned about their prospects of a sustainable retirement; in the background is the knowledge that the strength of their pension funds lies in the prosperity of the market, and custody is increasingly part of that market. And even if it sounds far-fetched to suggest that money and its power should so enter the jury room, there is no question that the presence of an increasingly sizeable commercial sector dealing in custody on the state's behalf will be part of what biases the body politic against any serious attempt to reduce the use of custody in our society. If the jury room is not influenced – yet – by the power money exercises, it is certain legislators are.

So it is that the effective sovereign power as it is now exercised by money shows few signs that the democratic controls which are enshrined in our constitutional arrangements are equal to the task of resisting what money and its holders are in an increasing position to demand. This is not, of course, to say that the exercise of democracy, of determining the will of the people by political processes and by the exercise of the vote, is not a crucially important aspect of our common life: it is to make the point that in the context of the growth in the power of money and the weight it carries in decision-making the traditional arrangements that belong to the exercise of democracy are increasingly ranged against forces too powerful for them. Buying votes may be the wrong side of the law; but we must be under no illusions about what can be achieved when money is able to change the desires of the people. As Dominy observes, markets and the money which drives them have to keep growing if the debt which is the basis of money is to be serviced, that is, if the financial sector, increasingly important as it is, is to prosper. To achieve that growth it is necessary to lock society into enlarging its desires for that which in the end does not satisfy.[8] As Pat Logan observes in the study undertaken on behalf of the Council of Churches of Britain and Ireland, *A World Transformed*:

> Capitalism must change. That is not an expression of a moral imperative. It is a comment on the very nature of capitalism itself. If it is to expand, or even to survive, ways of financing, producing and marketing must change as capitalists seek to gain and retain the competitive edge on one another. Ways of behaving must change as capitalists respond to the wishes of consumers, the demands of shareholders and the requirements of the state.[9]

In keeping with that, he describes capitalism as a 'regime'. In our terms it means that money is now, in its quantity, its volatility and in its capacity to organise the desires of society and individuals, sovereign. But that sovereignty does not simply lie in the way in which money has become the principal instrument of control in the UK – it is in the nature of money as it has become that it has extended its power *internationally*, to the point that national frontiers are no longer the barrier to its expansion. The international system of order still professes respect for the integrity of national territories, and national governments are condemned if they interfere in the affairs of their neighbours; not so with the power of money. In its exercise of sovereign power it shows no such respect; money rules not just at home but worldwide.

Power, sovereignty and church

No comment on power and the way in which the power of money has so vastly increased would be complete without a brief reflection on the effect this has on the place of the Church in society, not least in a nation where a national church has, through the mechanism of establishment, a sense of particular involvement in legislation and government. The claims for establishment and the defensiveness in the face of change are almost certainly exaggerated, and the claims for disestablishment likewise. Both sides in that debate also ignore the fact that the processes of attrition which have already diminished establishment will certainly continue and probably contain much that is good and hopeful. In the process there are new and exciting things to be learned and from time to time what we deem to be destructive aberrations to be challenged – after we've considered the case. Such an environment is challenging, but to a people who are heirs to the promise of the Spirit who leads into all the truth surely it is not to be seen as regrettable; it is after all in the *truth* that we seek to be established. Perhaps one by-product of the history of establishment that we do need to lose is a tendency to combine a negative reaction to change with a lack of forthrightness about real injustice.

The predominant thrust of this book's argument, however, means focusing attention on an aspect of establishment that is absolutely central but frequently overlooked, namely that it is about a relationship with *the sovereign*. The sovereign, as holder of the power to declare states of exception, specifically to exercise increasing power over the bare life of the subject, to lock up, to exclude and to grant or refuse basic rights of survival, is the one with whom an established church is in relation. That being so, what has caused a significant loss of effectiveness in the mechanism of establishment is the historic change to the location of sovereign power from the structures of the nation state to those who have control over money and the operation of the market. A debate about whether to change the relationship of the Church to the nation state ignores the more challenging issue of the Church's relation – or non-relation – to the market. It is there that the policies of nation states are increasingly determined, there that people are reduced to poverty or otherwise excluded from the mainstream of society.

Any consideration of the Church's relation to the state requires, therefore, that it take seriously the absence of any effective relationship with the sources of financial power or therefore with those able to affect for good and ill those experiencing poverty and exclusion. As the next chapter will show, it is also necessary to attend to the *international* character of those current sources of sovereign power, determining as they do the operation of a globalised market. We are not at liberty to ignore that historic development or simply to bemoan it; the divine project has always been, and is now, a global one, and there is too much on offer and too much at stake for us to neglect the opportunities or the challenges of that globalisation.

But as things are, the Church is perceived, and accurately so, as lacking both the determination or the skills to engage those who operate in the globalised financial marketplace, and at the same time the willingness to act in solidarity with those whom the international market subjects to states of exception. To remedy that is to embark on the reform of our discipleship, always a more challenging and demanding task than debating or even executing changes in our institutional arrangements. But the combination of the crisis of 2008, the explosion of frustration at the market's exercise of sovereign power represented by the Occupy movement, and the evidence that financial sector professionals do not believe that the Church has any useful ethical guidance to offer[10] – these and many other signs leave us no choice if we are to be faithful than to seek to address the global sovereign power of money, its controllers and its victims.

And believers are required to consider what has happened to sovereign power not least because of their claim to be following the one who resisted sovereign power to the point of becoming its victim, and of their declared conviction that he is the one to whom sovereignty ultimately belongs.

Notes

[1] David Marquand, *Mammon's Kingdom: An Essay on Britain, Now* (Allen Lane, 2014), p. 2.

[2] Peter Dominy, *Decoding Mammon* (Wipf & Stock, 2012), p. 102.

[3] Giorgio Agamben, *Homo Sacer: Sovereign Power and Bare Life* (Stamford University Press, 1998). For a fuller account of Agamben's thesis and of its relation to the 'sovereignty of the crucified Son of God', see my 'Reigning from the Tree – Reflections on the Sovereignty of the Crucified', Presidential Address to the Society for the Study of Theology, 2003.

[4] Quoted in Carl Schmitt, *Politische Theologie*; see Agamben, *Homo Sacer*, p. 16.

[5] Hannah Arendt, *Essays in Understanding, 1930–1954*, ed. Jerome Kohn (Harcourt & Brace, 1994); cf. Agamben, *Homo Sacer*, p. 120.

[6] See conference papers, Lambeth Conference 1998, available at http://www.lambethconference.org/1998/.

[7] *Guardian*, 25 April 2012.

[8] Dominy, *Decoding Mammon*, p. 96.

[9] Pat Logan, *A World Transformed* (CTBI, 2008), p. 131.

[10] See *Value and Values*, a report on the values of financial sector professionals by the St Paul's Institute: http://www.stpaulsinstitute.org.uk. For a fuller discussion of the nature of establishment, see my *Misestablishment*, the Eric Symes Abbott Lecture 2012 (see http://westminster-abbey.org).

4

From sovereignty to empire – sovereignty *sans frontière*

In our own day, the state finds itself having to address the limitations to its sovereignty imposed by the new context of international trade and finance, which is characterised by increasing mobility both of financial capital and means of production, material and immaterial. This new context has altered the political power of states.

Benedict XVI[1]

Posters advertising *The Spectator* on the London underground recently expressed in chilling terms the current nature of sovereign power: 'Most Germans own a second property', the poster proclaims: 'Greece'. The reality of sovereign power as it is exercised in a nation, Greece (which, we should not forget, is the cradle of European democracy), is that while the outward structures might indeed be more or less in place, rule of a quite different kind is being exercised, even if not with the violent brutality that we associate with the totalitarian regimes of the twentieth century. But from the point of view of the Greek people, and especially of its poor, any suggestion that their democracy exercises sovereignty in their country can only elicit a hollow laugh. For power over the population is being exercised in the context of the eurozone crisis by those who make financial decisions on behalf of the eurozone about the basis on which a bailout will be offered to the failing Greek banking system; so we see the spectacle of crowds of people unemployed as a result of the redundancies imposed particularly on the public sector, public disturbances in which the threat of violence is ever present, and widespread destitution. Failure to accede to the demands of the financial authorities in Brussels, in practice the bankers of the most powerful European economies, would entail a refusal on behalf of those bankers to bail out Greek banks and ultimately the Greek economy. Of course, it was a possible option to end Greece's membership of the eurozone, and many Greeks, faced with the conditions being offered by the eurozone's banks for a bailout, were quite openly proposing a return to Greece's own currency, the drachma. But that would not be cost-free: leaving the eurozone would entail serious devaluation of the Greek currency and the continuing shadow of debts from the past.

The pressure of such externally imposed conditions is not a new development. Countries in the two-thirds world are well used to the structural adjustment programmes that were imposed by the World Bank as a condition of alleviating their debts. They know well what it is like to be in the position where you have to spend more on servicing your nation's debts than you are allowed to spend on educating your nation's children or treating their illnesses. They know well also from bitter experience what happens to a nation overwhelmed by debt, and the distortions of international trade and national economies brought about by such stipulations – all made in the name of recreating a sound economy in which they trusted.[2]

As is well known, Greece was far from being the only country which found itself under economic direction from the authorities of the eurozone. and this erosion of national sovereignty did not end with Greece. Travelling a little further towards the periphery of the eurozone brings you to the island of Cyprus, and that island nation is experiencing not just one but two occupations. A visit to the Tomb of St Barnabas, one of the original Apostles and the patron saint of Cyprus, should not be especially complicated; but as things stand, when the members of the Synod of the Anglican Diocese of Cyprus and the Gulf met in Larnaca it was indeed extremely so: as well as a moment of touching base with our earliest Christian history, it created an exposure to the reality of Cyprus's current situation. The outing was scheduled as a morning trip to Famagusta, in the Turkish-occupied north of the island, where the

Synod Eucharist was to be held, and where we were to visit St Barnabas' tomb on the way.

But 'on the way' makes it sound too simple. Elaborate negotiations with 'the authorities' were needed to obtain the various permissions required for that journey. Then as the coach proceeded we had to enter the British sovereign base area, a relic of the independence negotiations that had led to Cypriot independence, and then cross into the Turkish-occupied part of the island, through a buffer zone overseen by United Nations peacekeepers. So far, three occupiers, and counting: Turkey with 35,000 troops, and the British and UN contingents with a far smaller number; but all signalling that the Government of the Republic of Cyprus is far from master in its own house. These forgotten occupations have continued through getting on for five decades.

But now has come in addition the worst of the occupations. The eurozone's requirements of Greece in exchange for the bailout of their economy have been mentioned above, involving as they did the virtual suspension of democracy in the country that is the cradle of European democracy. But a little-noticed aspect of that decision was its effect on the Cyprus banking system: the 'haircut' required of the Greek depositors involved Cypriot banks to a large extent, and the time bomb under the Cypriot economy started ticking.

It is frequently said that the Cyprus situation is unusual, that it doesn't set a precedent, because it had 'allowed itself' to have a banking system so much larger than the whole of the rest of the Cypriot economy. But what is this 'allowing itself'? A small, peripheral economy beyond the edge of continental Europe suddenly becomes highly attractive as a place of investment, and is encouraged to accept that inflow of funds so that prosperity could cascade downwards from its banks. Like the countries of the two-thirds world in the 1970s, offered huge loans at low interest, only to discover too late that times would change and debt would as a result become unsustainable, so Cyprus now has discovered, too late, that the money that enabled prosperity was actually merciless money. The prosperity was a bubble, and when it burst all that

would be said was how unwise it had been of the Cyprus banks to
be allowed to get so big.

If the complaint that Cypriot banks had got too big sounds
at all familiar, it is because it is precisely what was said in 2008
about British banks, and about an economy too dependent on
the financial sector. It is a feature of the financial sector (a weasel
expression, because it allows us to forget that 'the financial sector'
consists of human beings making decisions) that it is delighted to
grow in good times, and is then totally merciless and un-self-critical
when things crash.

Like so much of Europe in living memory, Cyprus found itself
caught between the power of Germany and the power of Russia,
and as the crisis unfolded the President of Cyprus was compelled
to shuttle between Moscow and Berlin begging for help, and being
told in both places that while they had been happy to pour money
into Cyprus in the good times, they were not to expect any support
now that things had deteriorated.

Naturally, under such external pressure it is only too likely
that mistakes have been made by those responsible for the Cypriot
economy; in particular there were Cypriot economists who foresaw
what was likely to take place, only to find their warnings going
unheeded. But what has been the outcome for this small island
with its venerable history and tormented story of occupier after
occupier controlling its destiny in their own interests?

The distressing but honest answer to that question is that the
outcome is indeed another 'occupation', and one that will make all
the other occupations last even longer. This new occupation is by
foreign banks, who dictate to the Cypriot authorities what are the
terms under which it will be allowed to survive at all – shades of
the quisling regimes in Nazi-occupied countries and the Russian-
authorised regimes of eastern Europe. And the survival on offer
is little more than that. The decision to tax even small depositors,
now rescinded, is being seen as a *tactical* error, underestimating
the psychological effect of taking money out of ordinary people's
bank accounts. Instead, deposits that are the lifeblood of Cyprus'
real economy, the capital that businesses need to function, are to

be taxed more heavily with the consequence of bankruptcies and unemployment.

And as the bankers 'occupy' their country, Cypriots can be sure that the other occupiers – in particular the Turkish army dividing the island – will stay yet longer, yet more likely to be forgotten by the world as the part of the island they occupy will seem to be a safer place for investment, in that it is effectively outside the eurozone. So the occupations support each other. A small island with a long experience of occupations by one power and another has become now a picture of a world occupied by money.

And when national economies with more money seek to avoid their money becoming subject to such transnational power it is not so as to challenge money's international sovereign power but rather to make sure that their economy will not become subject to the needs of the poorest who might be able to gain from access to their wealth. Speaking realistically, of course, everyone knows that any thought there might have been of the UK joining the eurozone is nowhere near to being on the political agenda. The fashionable view is that the whole euro project was a disaster or, as successive British governments have said, has an irresistible logic about it that leads to fiscal and economic union, and beyond that probably to political union as well. They have taken that view, no doubt, because of a desire to encourage the eurozone countries to grasp that logic – as the powerful German economy also wants the eurozone to do, as the only route to stabilise the beleaguered currency and put an end to emergency bailouts. For the German government that is an attractive way of increasing economic and political power and seems justified as they have to produce money to bail out failing banks elsewhere.

But a British government of whatever political persuasion will have another reason also for pointing to the logic that says that currency union requires political union: it is a convenient way of adding to the weight of argument against the UK ever joining the single currency: 'who wants to be part of a political united Europe?' is the unspoken question, with the clear assumption that the answer will be an overwhelming 'nobody' from the British electorate. It is politically helpful too in the argument against Scottish independence: 'if you leave the UK', the argument runs, 'you won't be independent at all; you'll have to join the euro, and Scotland, so far from being independent, will be tied into a European super-state.' So the politicians have spoken: the Scots can't have it both ways. They can stay in the UK and 'keep the pound' – one of the most successful currencies in history, we are being told. Or they can leave, in which case they have their own currency, and can't expect to be part of a currency union in which they continue to have a share in its governance.

There we have it: being an independent country (as the Scottish referendum voting paper has it) means having a currency you control – and it doesn't mean having the right to a say in someone else's. Sharing currency means sharing control and (again, politicians tell us) the story of the euro shows that you can't share a currency if you don't pool sovereignty. So if Scotland wants to end its sharing of sovereignty with England, Wales and Northern Ireland it is now being told that it won't share their currency either.

But such arguments take no account of the developments described in Chapter 2 that have affected profoundly what money has become. If we say, with Felix Martin, that money is not a 'thing' but can most appropriately be described as a 'set of ideas', then on the one hand money carries sovereign authority, and only the sovereign can create money that is 'legal tender'. But on the other hand, what happens if the people who use the money don't accept the authority of the sovereign? After all, if money is not a 'thing' you use to replace the world of barter – a world which has never existed – then it is rather that something becomes money if you trust it. A government can preside over a 'currency union' if – and only if – the people whom it governs *trust* the money which they authorise. Money is *credit*, and *credit* has its roots in 'trust'. For something to be trusted as money it has to be able to be tendered in exchange for goods or services in the confidence that it will be received and can then be handed on to others in turn in exchange for different goods and services. A government may say, with the forces of law and order behind their statements, that only pounds sterling will be accepted in payment of taxes and debts to the government. But what no government can do is force people to trust the coins, notes and entries in ledgers just because the government says so or prevent them recognising forms of currency that they find convenient and trustworthy.

If the people stop trusting the money the state gives them to use – as happens, for instance, when hyperinflation sets in – they will stop using it and use something else instead. The UK has resolutely refused to join the eurozone; it has insisted on controlling its own money, printing its own notes, validating its own currency. But that didn't stop euros trading freely in Belfast when it suited local traders to accept transactions entered into by people from the Irish Republic. To take another example, Uzbekistan is a country which shows quite clearly what happens when a population refuses to trust the currency proffered to them by their government: they stop using it, at least for major transactions such as house purchase, and use US dollars instead. The Uzbek people are quite happy to use Uzbek soums for transactions in the vegetable market; but when it comes to buying and selling houses, it has to be US dollars. And if a people decides to use US dollars for large transactions that effectively means that it is the US dollar that has to be there to back the Uzbek soum – because once it is known that there aren't enough dollars in reserve to back the soum nobody will use soums any more. Money is money when people trust it, and it isn't money when they cease to do so.

So there is a fundamental democracy – or perhaps we should coin the word *democredit* instead – about the status of a currency. The currency of a country is what the people trust; and what they cease to trust will no longer serve as currency. The tragedy through which we have passed of late is quite simply that the people have been persuaded to hand over their 'credit', the trust they place in their currency, to a small plutocratic elite, the proprietors of the banks. And when the banks failed, government rightly saw that what was at stake was nothing less than the trust of the people in their currency, and with that the ability to trade at all.

What that shows is that in the process of debating the possibility – or not – of a currency union based on the pound sterling the Scottish people might discover that they have in fact two votes to cast about Scottish independence. Alongside the political question of whether Scots trust the other parts of the UK to run their country and pass laws for it there is another question: whom will they trust with their money – not just trust to have it and spend it, but trust actually to create it? The politicians might just discover that once one side or the other has won the political battle that will be decided at the referendum there will be another, perhaps not immediate, vote that will take place, as the Scots decide which government they really trust with the most important thing they need a government to be trusted with – their money.

Arguments that are offered for retaining 'our' government's control over 'our' money gain support from the sense that if economic times demand it we can devalue, or allow the markets to do that for us, and so promote our competitiveness in world trade. They are given credibility by the spectacle of Greece and Cyprus, along probably with Italy and Spain ('the south') suffering the consequences of what is claimed to be their profligacy, their living on inflated debt. This is a version of the common enough perception that when it comes to the gap between rich and poor it is the poor who are the problem, and when it comes to indebtedness it is those who owe little who are 'living on debt' (the truth is that it is the wealthy who borrow the most and who live on debt the most also).

Underneath these arguments, highly questionable as they are even in their own terms, is a form of voluntarism which it is very tempting for the comfortably off to espouse, and has a particular temptation for those who hold religious convictions. That 'voluntarism' is the belief that it is morally better to be generous or charitable out of what is seen as a spontaneous and free choice than to make systemic adjustments that will take 'freedom of choice' away. Even if it can be shown – as it surely can be – that only *systemic changes* produce adequate benefits for the poor, the affluent will resist those adjustments in the belief that they must have the right to choose whom to help, how much to offer, when and on what terms. Such 'free' choices are more virtuous, the argument runs, than having a system which is more effective but at the cost (to the affluent) of taking away the sense of free choice.

The fashionable political consensus for the present is that we should be grateful for not being part of the euro, for having the freedom which having our own currency gives us to manage our own economy, and so not to be dragged down by the impoverished and indebted countries of southern Europe. There are three points to be made about this: it is as a result of not being in the eurozone that we are not tied into the lives and needs of Europe's poorest citizens: we are able to exhort them, even to condemn them; but we are not tied in with them, and they are not part of our lives as they would be if their economic and political decisions had actual perceptible effects on us.

Secondly, ultimately we *are* tied into the fate of the poor – not in fact just the poor of southern Europe but of the world: the pressure to be generous comes not just from altruism but from the accurate perception that a world in which some are too poor to survive is not going to be a good world for any of us. We are one with another; this is a small planet and we manage its resources together or we shall not manage them at all.

Thirdly, however economically attractive our position apart from the eurozone's crisis may appear at present, a week is a long time in economics, not just in politics. Who would dare say that in a world in which China, India and Brazil will rival the largest economies the time might not come, sooner than we perhaps think, when we shall be in the position of a Greece or even of a Chad or a Congo, when we would be only too glad if those in positions of economic power saw themselves as *bound in* with us and sharing our fate, and not simply helping us when they chose, and ignoring us when it suited. Times change, and with the change may well come an altered perception. Would it not be better to mount the argument for systems of real solidarity now while we have the choice?

For as we have seen, the shift in sovereign power is a global and not simply a national phenomenon. Nation states have less and less capacity to act as though they could exercise independent sovereignty. The globalisation of the market economy means that international finance determines more and more policies and outcomes over which nations have less and less control, and the scale of the global economy means that a dominant individual national economy can exercise enormous influence over the economies of other nations, and particularly over the poorest. What we have seen, and shall continue to see more and more, is the mutation of *sovereignty* into *empire*, sovereignty exercised without frontiers, sovereign power exercised through the vastly increased power of money. As Richard Barnet and John Cavanagh put it in their trenchant analysis of 'Electronic Money and the Casino Economy', in words reminiscent of those used by Pope Benedict XVI and quoted at the beginning of this chapter, 'The rise of global financial markets makes it increasingly difficult for national governments to formulate economic policy, much less to enforce it.'[3]

Unlike the empires of old, this empire is not the result of successful national imperialism but of financial power, supported by force where necessary but mostly exercised through the operation of the market and by the will of those with the most power to act there. As Michael Hardt and Antonio Negri put it in *Empire*, their account of this development:

> The passage to Empire emerges from the twilight of modern sovereignty. In contrast to imperialism, Empire establishes no territorial centre of power and does not rely on fixed boundaries or barriers. It is a decentered and deterritorializing apparatus of rule that progressively incorporates the entire global realm within its open, expanding frontiers.[4]

What this comes to mean for sovereign states they sum up bluntly:

> Today a notion of politics as an independent sphere of the determination of consensus and a sphere of mediation among conflicting social forces has very little room to exist. Consensus is determined more significantly by economic factors, such as the equilibria of the trade balances and speculation on the value of currencies.[5]

Without question, in the European context, it is the governments of the southern countries – Greece, Cyprus, Portugal, Spain – that are blamed for the crisis now affecting the eurozone, just as it is the poorest countries worldwide that are most frequently singled out for being the source of the corruption or mismanagement that is seen as the cause of their countries' difficulties. The world's poorest populations are indeed told to attribute their famine and disease to decisions made by their own government in the exercise of its sovereignty, or they may assume they are part of the givenness of their lives, rooted in climatic conditions or other matters beyond human control. No doubt those elements play a part. But in the main, and with the perspective of our examination of sovereign power over bare life, the reality is that the power of those who control money in the wealthiest countries has declared a 'state of exception' over the majority of humankind, and also gained the right to determine the law under which trading relations (and consequent relationships of credit and debt) exist.

As with most exercises of sovereign power, it is natural for the powerful to convince themselves that the course of action they take is also the most beneficial, not just for them but for those whose destiny they are deciding. They live out the closing sentence of Jesus' comment on the disciples' dispute about which of them is to be greatest: 'The kings of the Gentiles lord it over them; and those in authority over them are called benefactors.' (Luke 22.25)

The laws of the market that declare various states of exception and call them beneficial have much wider effects too. The global market has the potential to govern the whole environment of a society, its provision of health care and its educational system, its legal apparatus and criminal law. This is the other aspect of money's dominance, alongside its rule over those areas of people's lives declared to be 'private'.[6]

This account of the development of money as sovereign in a global context will of course provoke the response that there are also far more positive things to be said about globalisation than that it causes the most vulnerable people and nations to be excluded from human flourishing. The point will be made that it is not just an inevitable trend but one with many beneficial effects. From the standpoint of a Christian tradition which speaks again and again of the determination of God that God's love should be shared to the ends of the earth, we should not place ourselves among those who simply grumble about globalisation. It is quite true that there has been and continues to be a sharing of democratic institutions and the rule of law, ideals of solidarity and inclusion.

The issue is not whether good things have been shared around the world because of the process of globalisation, nor whether the technological advances that have produced the volatility of 'electronic money' do not also bring enormous benefits and opportunities with them. Rather, it is whether we can discover the means whereby the form of that globalisation brought about by the changed character and vastly increased power of money can be tamed. That question is being asked by many in the financial world itself, those who take seriously what the global crisis of 2008 may have to teach us. Stephen Green, for instance, with the experience of heading up a major international bank and serving in government behind him, observes:

> After 2008–2009, the manifest failure of market fundamentalism and the need for a re-balancing of the world's economy will inevitably be the starting point for a new world order, which will profoundly change international relationships. There may be some hard-core faithful who continue to believe that business as usual will be resumed, but the consensus is that – as the former Fed chairman and market fundamentalist Alan Greenspan has acknowledged – there was to say the least a 'flaw' in the model. Society the world over demands remorse from the practitioners and action from the politicians.[7]

It is salutary to reflect that the benefits that globalisation has shared exhibit the same inequalities that were in place before it gathered the pace to which we are now accustomed. Democratic institutions, inclusion, the rule of law – these as well as the more material benefits of global technology – seem to be distributed in a way that enhances rather than mitigates the gap between rich and poor nations.

The argument being offered here is that this enhancement rather than mitigation of inequality, alongside other negative results of globalisation, derives from a failure to address the principal driving force behind the globalisation process, and that is the place in which sovereign power has come to reside – in money itself. The vastly increased volatility and quantity of money has led to the acquisition of sovereign power – *vitae necisque potestas*, the power of life and death, which in turn means the ultimate power of decision in human affairs – by money itself. Not subject to the authority of governments but generated instead by private institutions for their own profit, it is money that holds the power in the determining of national and international priorities. Stephen Green's call for 'remorse from practitioners and action from politicians' will amount to very little if this fundamental point is not grasped. We shall continue to live in what Richard Barnet and John Cavanagh call 'the increasingly anarchic world of high speed money'[8] without realising why the world has become that way: subject, as money is, only to the speculative aims of those generating money for their own profit, no attempts at the regulation of bankers' behaviour will hold this anarchy at bay, for anarchy is of the essence of what money requires for it to gain profit for the individuals and corporate bodies which create it.

This is the paradox of sovereign anarchy: immensely powerful yet acting only on its own uncontrolled instinct to produce more of itself. And it is at this point that the question has to be asked, what is it that makes money and its sovereign power so immune from challenge? What lies behind the sense that it is that about which no questions can be asked? What is it that makes governments quake at the prospect of any disruption in the sovereign power of money?

It is perhaps not surprising that, in the quotation above, Stephen Green, himself an ordained priest and clearly given to theological reflection on this topic, should speak of some supporters of unrestricted globalisation as 'hard-core faithful' and 'market fundamentalists'; what is perhaps of greater interest is that the language of 'Mammon's reign' and 'Mammon worship' should appear in the writing of a professed unbeliever, David Marquand.[9] While he does not examine what it might mean to give money the name of a divinity or characterise society's commitment to being ruled by Mammon as 'worship', could it perhaps be that the language has surfaced out of a subconscious recognition that the source of this 'reign' and the reluctance to challenge it lies in the fact that it has acquired the status of a deity? If we are to examine that possibility it is first necessary to consider what an *idol* is, and what is the nature of the divinities which idols represent. Perhaps we might discover that finding a remedy for the situation in which we find ourselves requires a consideration of the wisdom which led in the past to idols being identified and dethroned.

Notes

1   Benedict XVI, *Caritas in Veritate* (Vatican Press, 2009), para.,24.
2   It has often been said that the difficulties of the Greek economy did not originate with the eurozone bailout conditions, but with the past mismanagement of the Greek economy. That has often been said about economies which are subjected to external conditions. My point is not with allocating blame but with the present situation in which Greek people find themselves. See also Susan George, *A Fate Worse than Debt* (Penguin, 1988) and her many other accounts of the effects of unrepayable debt on the lives of indebted nations and on the international economy. See also Chapter 5 of my *Grace and Mortgage* (Darton, Longman & Todd, 1997, 2009), pp. 73–93.
3   Richard Barnet and John Cavanagh, 'Electronic Money and the Casino Economy' in Edward Goldsmith and Jerry Mander (eds.), *The Case Against the Global Economy* (Earthscan, 2001), p. 67.
4   Michael Hardt and Antonio Negri, *Empire* (Harvard University Press, 2000), p. xii.
5   Hardt and Negri, Empire, p. 307.
6   Michael Sandel asks, with numerous examples to back up his case, what if anything is left that money can't buy. See Michael Sandel, *What Money Can't Buy: The Moral Limits of Markets* (Allen Lane, 2012).
7   Stephen Green, *Good Value* (Allen Lane, 2009), p. 125. The book marks a very significant change of tone from his earlier *Serving God, Serving Mammon* (Marshall Pickering, 1996), which suggests a much easier accommodation between the demands of 'serving God' and 'serving Mammon'.
8   Barnet and Cavanagh, 'Electronic Money and the Casino Economy', p. 67.
9   David Marquand, *Mammon's Reign* (Allen Lane, 2014), where references to 'worship' appear frequently; see for example p. 51.

5

What is an idol?

Not to us, O LORD, not to us, but to your name give glory,
  for the sake of your steadfast love and your faithfulness.
Why should the nations say, 'Where is their God?'
Our God is in the heavens; he does whatever he pleases.
Their idols are silver and gold, the work of human hands.
They have mouths, but do not speak; eyes, but do not see.
They have ears, but do not hear; noses, but do not smell.
They have hands, but do not feel; feet, but do not walk;
  they make no sound in their throats.
Those who make them are like them;
  so are all who trust in them.
O Israel, trust in the LORD! He is their help and their shield.
O house of Aaron, trust in the LORD! He is their help and their
  shield.
You who fear the LORD, trust in the LORD! He is their help and
  their shield.
The LORD has been mindful of us; he will bless us;
  he will bless the house of Israel; he will bless the house of Aaron;
  he will bless those who fear the LORD, both small and great
May the LORD give you increase, both you and your children.
May you be blessed by the LORD, who made heaven and earth.
The heavens are the LORD's heavens,
  but the earth he has given to human beings.
The dead do not praise the LORD,
  nor do any that go down into silence.
But we will bless the LORD from this time on and for evermore.
Praise the LORD!

Psalm 115

To write 'idol' in the title of a book is to take a risk, as it is to speak of 'idolatry'. After all, 'idol' is now common parlance, used in all sorts of ways: celebrities are referred to as 'idols'; some parents 'idolise' their children. So to speak of an 'idol' might lead the reader to think of anyone or anything regarded as wonderful, faultless, exciting or worth paying a great deal to go and see.

There's another risk in referring to an idol: the word might take the reader's mind into a realm of the arcane or the primitive: exotic shrines or statuettes of the kind you can buy in tourist shops. Read from that perspective, the copious biblical material on idols and idolatry looks like an account of another world, a world of competing deities, strange rituals and gruesome sacrifices. That is a world, we would wish to persuade ourselves, which we have long since ceased to inhabit, and certainly not one that could have anything much to do with the running of a modern economy.[1]

Yet we need to exercise caution before consigning idols and idolatry to a world long passed or allowing its seamless translation into our modern world of social media and celebrity cults. For the idols and the deities they represented need to be approached with respect as the articulation by ancient peoples of their response to life forces they faced with awe and wonder, and which they could not control. Thus that polytheistic account of the world and the religious responses to which it gave rise played a crucial role in giving meaning to a world that was uncertain in its processes and truly daunting in what pain it might inflict. Seen in that way, far from being remote from our experience, the idols and the world view in which they figured arose from an experience of which we are also aware: we do not differ overmuch from our ancestors in the need to make order out of a disturbing environment and to express in ritual action and in art as well as words some sense of meaning in a life and an environment which often seem to be totally meaningless.

If the suggestion that the world of idols and idolatry needs to be approached with 'respect' seems strange, perhaps even outrageous, that is because we are apt to confuse the ferocity with which idolatry is condemned in the Old and New Testaments with a sense that they are of no account or consequence. On the contrary, however, that ferocious condemnation is precisely a recognition of an attractiveness in the polytheistic world and its three-dimensional representations that is both constant and compelling. The impulse to turn to the cults of surrounding nations as a source of security was ever-present, never more so than when the Hebrew people faced imminent danger. What might to modern eyes seem like resort to political alliances and 'diplomatic' or political activity to safeguard the life of the nation was also intrinsically of religious significance: intermarriage, as well as being politically expedient, often meant the establishment of some status for the religion of the nation with which an alliance was being forged, along with the introduction of its cults and shrines.

Along with that came inevitably the cultural and political arrangements that were validated by the cult, the 'world view', we might say, of the nation in question. Of the attractiveness of other nations' ways of life and what in modernity would be regarded as their religious expression we can be in no doubt: their absolute and unconditional monarchies, validated by the cults of deities from which the king was often believed to be descended, were attractive in times of uncertainty, far more attractive often than the austere demands of the God of Israel. To serve that God the Hebrew people had to be content with a monarch that was subject to moral constraints, and with observances that were intimately linked to the covenant relationship they had with God, a relationship that was characterised by a range of severe moral demands, covering every aspect of life, with dire sanctions if those demands were not obeyed.

Key to that covenant was the people's recall of their escape from slavery, and therefore the requirement that they should not revert to customs and practices which were features of the slave life from which their ancestors had been rescued. Ceremonies of historical recall were therefore the hallmark of the Hebrew people's observances, celebrating the events that had brought the people into being. Those events – the Exodus and the wilderness wandering – had established the God of the Hebrew people as characterised by a commitment to the redeeming of the enslaved and the maintenance of a common life that was to be protected from a reversion to the nature of the slave society; after all, it was escape from that society which, as they recalled again and again, had established their identity.

However, the frequency with which the danger of idolatry and its disastrous consequences are referred to in the literature of the Hebrew people serves to make clear just how attractive, just how prevalent, were the attractions of myths and idolatrous practices. Every attempt to establish such cults in Israel recalled the archetypical event that established for all time the contrast between the religious observances and, we might say, the moral and political cultures of the nations and the covenant demands of God.

> Then Moses turned and went down from the mountain, carrying the two tablets of the covenant in his hands, tablets that were written on both sides, written on the front and on the back. The tablets were the work of God, and the writing was the writing of God, engraved upon the tablets. When Joshua heard the noise of the people as they shouted, he said to Moses, 'There is a noise of war in the camp.' But he said, 'It is not the sound made by victors, or the sound made by losers; it is the sound of revellers that I hear.'

> As soon as he came near the camp and saw the calf and the dancing, Moses' anger burned hot, and he threw the tablets from his hands and broke them at the foot of the mountain. He took the calf that they had made, burned it with fire, ground it to powder, scattered it on the water, and made the Israelites drink it.

> Moses said to Aaron, 'What did this people do to you that you have brought so great a sin upon them?' And Aaron said, 'Do not let the anger of my lord burn hot; you know the people, that they are bent on evil. They said to me, "Make us gods, who shall go before us; as for this Moses, the man who brought us up out of the land of Egypt, we do not know what has become of him." So I said to them, "Whoever has gold, take it off"; so they gave it to me, and I threw it into the fire, and out came this calf!'

When Moses saw that the people were running wild (for Aaron had let them run wild, to the derision of their enemies), then Moses stood in the gate of the camp, and said, 'Who is on the LORD's side? Come to me!' And all the sons of Levi gathered around him. He said to them, 'Thus says the LORD, the God of Israel, "Put your sword on your side, each of you! Go back and forth from gate to gate throughout the camp, and each of you kill your brother, your friend, and your neighbour."' The sons of Levi did as Moses commanded, and about three thousand of the people fell on that day. Moses said, 'Today you have ordained yourselves for the service of the LORD, each one at the cost of a son or a brother, and so have brought a blessing on yourselves this day.'

On the next day Moses said to the people, 'You have sinned a great sin. But now I will go up to the LORD; perhaps I can make atonement for your sin.' So Moses returned to the LORD and said, 'Alas, this people has sinned a great sin; they have made for themselves gods of gold. But now, if you will only forgive their sin – but if not, blot me out of the book that you have written.' But the LORD said to Moses, 'Whoever has sinned against me I will blot out of my book. But now go, lead the people to the place about which I have spoken to you; see, my angel shall go in front of you. Nevertheless, when the day comes for punishment, I will punish them for their sin.'

Then the LORD sent a plague on the people, because they made the calf – the one that Aaron made.

(Exodus 32.15–35)

So in a story remembered in subsequent generations the testing demands of the wilderness escape and the anxieties and privations it imposed led to a popular demand to embrace a more immediate cult around which they could gather, one that had the merit of visibility but also did not require the patience and moral commitment of the faith of the Hebrew people. The breaking of the stone tablets on which the covenant was inscribed, the requirement that the people drink the pulverised remnants of the idol, the slaughter that ensued – all this is to indicate beyond any possibility of forgetting the irreconcilable contrast between the faith to which the Hebrew people were committed and the world view and the practices of the surrounding nations.

The story echoed through subsequent crises. Ahab King of Israel forged an alliance with Sidon, sealed with his marriage to the daughter of the king and with the embracing of the Baal cult. The climactic confrontation between the two world views occurs on Mount Carmel, between Elijah and the Baal prophets: the account leaves no doubt about the nature of the cult, about its total failure, and about Elijah's scathing mockery of the characteristics of the divinity to whom they were sacrificing.

> So they took the bull that was given them, prepared it, and called on the name of Baal from morning until noon, crying, 'O Baal, answer us!' But there was no voice, and no answer. They limped about the altar that they had made. At noon Elijah mocked them, saying, 'Cry aloud! Surely he is a god; either he is meditating, or he has wandered away, or he is on a journey, or perhaps he is asleep and must be awakened.' Then they cried aloud and, as was their custom, they cut themselves with swords and lances until the blood gushed out over them. As midday passed, they raved on until the time of the offering of the oblation, but there was no voice, no answer, and no response.
>
> (1 Kings 18.26–29)

The narrative of Elijah's confrontation of Ahab and Jezebel makes very clear the relationship between the political crisis represented by that confrontation and the contrast between the religion of the God of Israel and the Baal cult which was part and parcel of Ahab's regime. Elijah is clear in that confrontation that it is Ahab's dereliction of the covenant with God that is the cause of the conflicts within his kingdom:

When Ahab saw Elijah, Ahab said to him, 'Is it you, you troubler of Israel?' He answered, 'I have not troubled Israel; but you have, and your father's house, because you have forsaken the commandments of the LORD and followed the Baals.

(1 Kings 18.17–18)

Any suggestion that the world of polytheistic religion, of deities and their myths, is remote from the world of politics and ethics is, so far as the biblical record is concerned, without foundation. Loyalty to the God of Israel requires a different pattern of life and political organisation from that which is associated with the ways of the nations and their gods. So when Israel demands of Samuel that they be provided with a king, a request made in order to give them strength against the surrounding nations, they are left in no doubt what is at stake; and the world of the idols and their corporate life are all of a piece.

Then all the elders of Israel gathered together and came to Samuel at Ramah, and said to him, 'You are old and your sons do not follow in your ways; appoint for us, then, a king to govern us, like other nations.' But the thing displeased Samuel when they said, 'Give us a king to govern us.' Samuel prayed to the LORD, and the LORD said to Samuel, 'Listen to the voice of the people in all that they say to you; for they have not rejected you, but they have rejected me from being king over them. Just as they have done to me, from the day I brought them up out of Egypt to this day, forsaking me and serving other gods, so also they are doing to you. Now then, listen to their voice; only – you shall solemnly warn them, and show them the ways of the king who shall reign over them.'

So Samuel reported all the words of the LORD to the people who were asking him for a king. He said, 'These will be the ways of the king who will reign over you: he will take your sons and appoint them to his chariots and to be his horsemen, and to run before his chariots; and he will appoint for himself commanders of thousands and commanders of fifties, and some to plough his ground and to reap his harvest, and to make his implements of war and the equipment of his chariots. He will take your daughters to be perfumers and cooks and bakers. He will take the best of your fields and vineyards and olive orchards and give them to his courtiers. He will take one-tenth of your grain and of your vineyards and give it to his officers and his courtiers. He will take your male and female slaves, and the best of your cattle and donkeys, and put them to his work. He will take one-tenth of your flocks, and you shall be his slaves. And in that day you will cry out because of your king, whom you have chosen for yourselves; but the Lord will not answer you in that day.'

(1I Samuel 8.4–18)

But the strengths of the 'other nations' and their pattern of life, including their gods, proved too attractive in the face of the national dangers they faced.

But the people refused to listen to the voice of Samuel; they said, 'No! but we are determined to have a king over us, so that we also may be like other nations, and that our king may govern us and go out before us and fight our battles.' When Samuel had heard all the words of the people, he repeated them in the ears of the LORD. The LORD said to Samuel, 'Listen to their voice and set a king over them.' Samuel then said to the people of Israel, 'Each of you return home.'

(1 Samuel 8.19–22)

God and the gods – ethics and politics

This contrast between the God of the Hebrews and the gods represented by the idols accounts for some of those aspects of biblical religion which present the modern mind with the greatest difficulty. Thus a sense of moral outrage rises in the present day believer when she reads, at the beginning of the story of the Flood:

> The LORD saw that the wickedness of humankind was great in the earth, and that every inclination of the thoughts of their hearts was only evil continually. And the LORD was sorry that he had made humankind on the earth, and it grieved him to his heart. So the LORD said, 'I will blot out from the earth the human beings I have created – people together with animals and creeping things and birds of the air, for I am sorry that I have made them.'
>
> (Genesis 6.5–8)

Our mind revolts against the punitive response to the immorality God observes, and in particular it revolts against the idea that the total destruction of the planet, including the animals and plants which have no responsibility for the violence God sees on the earth, might be divine punishment for the wickedness of humankind. This is only made more puzzling when, at the end of the story, when the waters have subsided and it is possible for Noah and his family and all the inhabitants of the ark to leave the ark and resume life on dry ground, God appears to change his mind yet again (even if this time in a way that accords more readily with what a modern reader might wish God to think):

> The LORD said in his heart, 'I will never again curse the ground because of humankind, for the inclination of the human heart is evil from youth; nor will I ever again destroy every living creature as I have done. As long as the earth endures, seedtime and harvest, cold and heat, summer and winter, day and night, shall not cease.'
>
> (Genesis 8.21–22)

If our conscience revolts against a deity who would destroy the created order out of a need to vindicate God's justice, there is in that opening statement a clear understanding that this catastrophe is rooted in *moral* judgement. At the same time, when the flood abates that moral judgement remains, but alongside the firmness of God's intention for the survival of humankind and the species committed to their care. So God affirms God's commitment to a covenant of hope:

> As for me, I am establishing my covenant with you and your descendants after you, and with every living creature that is with you, the birds, the domestic animals, and every animal of the earth with you, as many as came out of the ark. I establish my covenant with you, that never again shall all flesh be cut off by the waters of a flood, and never again shall there be a flood to destroy the earth.' God said, 'This is the sign of the covenant that I make between me and you and every living creature that is with you, for all future generations: I have set my bow in the clouds, and it shall be a sign of the covenant between me and the earth. When I bring clouds over the earth and the bow is seen in the clouds, I will remember my covenant that is between me and you and every living creature of all flesh; and the waters shall never again become a flood to destroy all flesh. When the bow is in the clouds, I will see it and remember the everlasting covenant between God and every living creature of all flesh that is on the earth.' God said to Noah, 'This is the sign of the covenant that I have established between me and all flesh that is on the earth.'
>
> (Genesis 9.9–17)

In a narrative with so many echoes of the many ancient stories of a primeval flood, what is critical here is the implied assertion that the event originates not in the outcomes of conflicts among deities, their passions, love affairs and rivalries, but in the essentially *moral* character of the God of the Hebrews. It is God's righteous moral anger that leads to the outpouring of the floodwaters and the destruction of the life that God had created; it is God's commitment to some continuation of the enterprise that is expressed in saving Noah and his family and the pair of each bird and animal, and then affirmed at the end of the story. God's 'change of heart' arises from that commitment to a continuing enterprise, established in the creation of all the species and of humankind in particular. Both the righteousness that led to the onset of the flood and the 'change of heart' in the two passages just quoted set the creation as being held in the care and claimed by the demand of a fundamentally moral deity. As Walter Brueggemann puts it:

> The entire narrative is concerned with the tension between God's will for and call to creation and the mixed way the creation heeds that will and answers that call. Informed by [Genesis] 8.20–22 and 9.8–17 we have found that the pathos of God is the clue to the movement of the flood narrative.[2]

This 'pathos of God' is rooted, as the Hebrew faith has it, in their immensely courageous insistence that the contradictory and disturbing experiences of life find their meaning not in the chaotic encounters of rival deities but in God's commitment to a will that created and a call that was directed to the world. To that will and that call creation responds in ways that are conflicting, and create at the centre of life a 'pathos', a tension between the righteousness demanded by God and the merciful commitment which leads to God's holding to that demand and that commitment, despite the confusing and conflicting responses that God receives.

The response that this will, this call and this commitment ask for is entirely different from that which would be asked for if the world were – as a polytheistic account would have it – the product of the chaotic encounters of sundry divinities. For all the attractiveness of that 'explanation' of life's unpredictability, it carries the implication that life is indeed a matter of humankind attempting to avert the disasters and secure the blessings it desired. Humankind's only option would essentially be to engage in a fearful and manipulative second guessing of heavenly forces.

On any reckoning, the decision made by our Hebrew ancestors to reject such a world view in favour of placing trust in the will, the call, the pathos that arise from seeing life as a moral, not an arbitrary, enterprise must be reckoned truly remarkable. That their history included repeated dereliction of that commitment and of the covenant response that it called for from them is less remarkable than that they made the commitment in the first place. It is that commitment – to that will, that call, that pathos – that informs the whole biblical record as well as the subsequent history of Christianity. It is what the 'new covenant' sealed with the sacrifice of Christ affirms anew. Again, the fact that the demand for trust and obedience prove time and again too much is a matter for penitence, but not surely for surprise: the blandishments of various apparent opportunities of achievement and security without the painful demands that trust makes upon a community of believers often prove too great to resist.

What was clear to our ancestors, however, is that whatever were the attractions of gods that were immediate and idols that were visible, the surrender to the chaos of the deities could only lead to chaos and destruction within the life of the society. For all the vagaries and twists of Hebrew history, there is a clarity about there being one God, one alone, who was at one and the same time the only source of order in the world and the only assurance of a social order in which the most vulnerable would be protected. The contrast is made very clear in another of the psalms:

> God has taken his place in the divine council;
>   in the midst of the gods he holds judgement:
> 'How long will you judge unjustly
>   and show partiality to the wicked?
> Give justice to the weak and the orphan;
>   maintain the right of the lowly and the destitute.
> Rescue the weak and the needy;
>   deliver them from the hand of the wicked.'
> They have neither knowledge nor understanding,
>   they walk around in darkness;
>   all the foundations of the earth are shaken.
> I say, 'You are gods,
>   children of the Most High, all of you;
>   nevertheless, you shall die like mortals,
>   and fall like any prince.'
>
>   (Psalm 82)

But the commitment stands. God's people were not – such is the call, the will by which humanity was created – to surrender their lives to some notion that all is best left to chance or to the might of the strong, those with power or wealth, just because they tell us that is the only way and we are too confused to see any other. This book has been written from the perspective, one to be described in more detail in the next chapter, that money and the goings on with it, for it and around it, have enough of the characteristics of the chaotic encounters of the divinities which Israel decided to exclude from its life to deserve to be called an idol, perhaps even the most powerful candidate to be credited with making the world go round. It has, I shall seek to show, much of the capacity to engender a sense of chaotic arbitrariness that polytheistic world views also engendered. It – money, Mammon – has encouraged us to believe that a sophisticated game of second guessing is the only sensible response to its fearful power, and that having more and more of it is the only wise ambition, the only security against a life of penury and misery, that we can imagine.

There is one further aspect of the character of idols and the worship of them which the biblical record enjoins upon us. It is that when something acquires the dominant place of a divinity in the life of a people, an object of worship, that will have an effect on the character of that people: they will participate in the characteristics of that which has become their object of worship: in the words from Psalm 115 that were quoted at the start of this chapter:

> They have mouths, but do not speak; eyes, but do not see.
> They have ears, but do not hear; noses, but do not smell.
> They have hands, but do not feel; feet, but do not walk;
>   they make no sound in their throats.
> Those who make them are like them;
>   so are all who trust in them.

(Psalm 115.5–8)

It is verse 8, 'Those who make them are like them; so are all who trust in them', that draws attention to the capacity of idols to 'form' their devotees, to 'make them like themselves'. As Martin Luther puts it in his exposition of the First Commandment in the *Large Catechism*, 'that ... upon which you set your heart and put your trust is properly your god'.[3] As G. K. Beale puts it in his examination of idolatry, *We Become What We Worship*,[4] those who follow idols come to share the inability to see, hear, touch and feel, which are the characteristics of the objects of worship made by human hands. As we shall see when we examine the way in which money functions as an idol, it shares with the idols that the psalmist condemns the characteristic of making those who follow it become like it.

The role of recall

This account of idols and the deities they represent shows clearly the courage and perceptiveness that characterised our ancestors in faith who regarded themselves as belonging to the true deity and therefore as released from the dominion of the rival deities of the surrounding cultures. They inhabited the same uncertain and capricious world as did their neighbours; they found themselves frequently besieged by nations far stronger than themselves. Nonetheless, they made a commitment to resisting the cults and rituals which appeared to give to those neighbours such superior strength in favour of a God who was unseen, who required of his worshippers immense patience in the face of adversity and obedience to a demanding ethical code. However frequently they had to admit that they failed in the demands which that commitment laid on them, they held to it, reiterated it, and when they had failed to honour it sought forgiveness and the possibility to return to it.

That is in fact the only basis on which we know the story of the Hebrew people's experience of idols, their attraction, the disastrous consequences of following after them and the possibility of return to the faith they professed. We know this story because there is preserved the record of those who had the courage to confront them with the truth, to recall them to their commitment, and to bear the cost of doing so. The prophetic tradition is a tradition of *recall*, carried on throughout the history of this community of faith. Their role was to remind and to remember; like the festivals observed by the people of Israel, they existed lest the attractiveness of the idols might go unchallenged, lest there be a forgetting of their roots as a people who had found freedom from slavery to a culture in which the deities represented by idols reigned supreme, and lest there be a disregarding of the consequences that had been visited upon their ancestors as a result of acts of faithlessness. That tradition of recall continued within the observances of the Christian community, in its hearing of the Scriptures with their narrative of the history and its rehearsing in sacramental worship of the decisive Word, God's offering of recall and grace to a community that was likewise tempted to repeat the derelictions of the past. We only know of the place of idols, of those who had fallen for their blandishments, of the merciful readiness of the true God to allow return – we only know these things because of the particular character of that God, one who welcomes those who return.

This tradition of recall means that what the next chapter has to say about the ways in which money has accrued to itself many of the characteristics of the idols will be able to include something else also: the possibility that the community of faith in this age might learn ways to repent of its following of money. In so doing it will rediscover the remarkable grace of the one who still demands patience and obedience, but who also offers mercy and grace. So it might indeed be possible that seeing money as *idol* would put this generation in touch with possibilities of change, restoration and hope.

Notes

1. As an example of, and introduction to, the range of material on this topic, see Susan Ackerman, 'Idol, Idolatry' in David Noel Freedman (ed.), *Erdmans Dictionary of the Bible* (Eerdmans, 2000), pp. 625–7.

2. Walter Brueggemann, *Genesis* (Westminster John Knox Press, 1986), p. 9.

3. Martin Luther, 'The First Commandment' in *Large Catechism* (1580). See Theodore G. Tappert (ed.), *The Book of Concord* (Fortress Press, 1959), p. 360.

4   G. K. Beale, *We Become What We Worship* (InterVarsity Press, 2008). Beale's
    exegesis of Isaiah 6 makes clear that he means that we become *like* what we
    worship. He has expressed this in his book title as a metaphor rather than a
    simile, for effect.

6

Money as an idol

The upholsterer eyed the antique chair and listed all that would need to be done to it to restore it to its former beauty and serviceability. He got his calculator out and worked out the price he would need to charge. He saw my face when he told me the figure. 'I know what you're thinking,' he said. 'You're thinking of those advertisements for an armchair that say you can have it now and only start paying in two years' time.' He got his calculator out again. 'Have you worked out what it costs them to offer you the two years interest free?' He worked it out, and looked up. 'If you take that off the price they're charging for the chair, what's left is the value of the chair you're buying. If you have me re-upholster your armchair all the money you pay goes into my work and the fabric. That's the difference. What he had just worked out was the price people were prepared to pay for impatience. That was in the boom years. That world changed in 2008.

Fantasy wealth

This book began outside a post office, with people queuing for National Lottery tickets. Just a few doors down is the window of one of the many estate agents that populate our high streets. There is a knot of people standing there, looking at pictures of properties. Some, no doubt, are looking for their next home, checking what is available. That's what estate agents are for, to match what is available with those who are looking for a home.

But a few conversations later, the picture is not so clear. Ask the bystanders whether they are thinking of moving house and a high proportion will answer 'no'. They're looking at houses like their own to see what their house is likely to be worth. They have read in the newspapers that house prices are far outstripping other elements of the cost of living, and they want to know how that is affecting the price that would be put on their house. Some have had a flurry of leaflets through their letter box from estate agents promising a high price and ready buyers, and they too want to check what that means in their case by comparing with the prices being asked by other sellers.

The odd thing about this scene is that what people are seeing is inflation, house prices going up, and going up fast. And as we all know, we are against inflation – it is a Bad Thing. It was worrying to the commentators that the Bank of England was taking so long to meet its inflation target, and it is with some relief that it is being observed that the rate of inflation has fallen to the point that it is no longer a major worry; the expectation is that the Bank of England will not have to take action to curb it. The traditional instruments used against inflation, restricting the money supply and raising interest rates, have been kept in the bottom drawer at the Bank of England for such a long time now that we hope that the rate of inflation will not cause them to have to use those instruments again.

Folk memories of inflation are still etched into the public mind, and that is why we continue to become anxious when we observe inflation that cannot be brought under control even in a period of recession. The Governor of the Bank of England is required to write to the Chancellor of the Exchequer every time the Bank's inflation target is missed, and he must by now be quite exhausted from thinking up new reasons to give in his letter of apology.

It is important to examine the roots of this basic inconsistency in the way we think about rising prices. For one of the ways in which we assess whether a recovery is happening is precisely the state of the housing market. If house prices are going up we are encouraged to be pleased: not just are homeowners enabled to borrow against the rising value of the property they live in, but the sense that your home is worth more than it was encourages 'consumer confidence', that most significant of requirements for economic growth. When consumers are 'confident', they go out and spend money (rather than saving it), and if their home is not rising in value they lose confidence and as a result hold on to their money, even though interest rates are at an all-time low.

It is more common to speak of 'rising house prices' than house-price inflation; and for rising house prices no apology is required. If cauliflowers and electricity become more expensive, questions are asked about how that inflation is to be eliminated; if the same happens to house prices there is general euphoria and a sense that this is a sign of prosperity. The euphoria is of course self-interested, the result of three decades of encouraging 'home ownership' (for which read mortgage debt). The number of us who 'own' our own homes (funded by debts to banks and building societies) now significantly exceeds those of us who rent our home (and who accordingly pay more in rents). More significant still is the fact that the 'owners' of property vastly outnumber those who *aspire* to be in that position, and who therefore are prevented from even starting out on the 'property ladder' by the inflation in property prices, especially in London. There are, that is to say, far more votes in rising house prices than falling ones.

So crocodile tears are wept over the plight of first-time buyers, but that is exactly what they are: crocodile tears. For it is well understood that the self-interest of the large majority of citizens lies precisely in the house-price inflation which makes life so difficult for those seeking to begin the process of owning a home. There is a generational issue too: many home owners find that their housing outgoings – interest and capital repayments – are minuscule in comparison with the prices their children and grandchildren find themselves having to pay. Meanwhile the middle aged look to the increase in house prices as the means of funding their future social care in old age while resenting the prospect of watching their parents having to sell their home – and reduce their expected inheritance – in order to fund their own social care.

What has happened is that in the boom years the readily available credit offered by banks and building societies is funnelled into a steady increase in the price of land, the real root of the

house-price inflation. As Mark Twain observed in relation to the
price of land, the price is bound to keep going up with demand
'because they aren't making it any more'. And there is already
widespread concern being expressed that adding more funds for
house-purchase lending aimed mainly at helping first-time buyers
may simply result in further house-price inflation: nothing will
be gained from easier credit for prospective first-time buyers if all
they see is that they have to pay more than they can afford for the
property in which they wish to live.

What, then, is money *doing* to the ability of people to house
themselves and their dependants? For in what money has become
it is no longer a neutral substance being deployed to buy a home.
Instead it has been turned into an actor, transforming the absolutely
essential task of enabling people to have a home into a process for
enabling people to acquire more of itself. The majority of those
looking into the windows of the local estate agent are in fact eyeing
the progress of what has become their principal *investment*, the main
means whereby people who will never earn the vast salaries of
bankers and chief executives or own vast fortunes in stocks and
shares can nonetheless acquire an asset worth a vast sum of money
and engage in a form of dealing which is normally only open to
the wealthy. Money, that is to say, has transformed their desire for a
home into a desire for wealth.

But in the process money is doing something else also,
exercising another powerful transformation. For those looking into
the estate agent's window will include some who are not seeking
wealth for its own sake but seeking to overcome their fear of a
poverty-stricken old age, one in which their possible need for long-
term residential care will need to be funded by the proceeds of this
asset. The cards in the window depict the transformation of the
land and the bricks and mortar that could be their home into an
insurance policy against future disaster.

Some will be looking at the cards in the window in order
to find a home; but what money has done is to attract these two
other groups of bystanders, those who see in their house a means
to unaccustomed wealth, and those who in fear and dread of future
penury see their house as something that when it has done its

duty as their home will realise the money that will stand between themselves and elderly years spent in privation and distress.

Into this complex situation of desire for wealth and fear for the future come those with a wish to find political solutions, preferably solutions that will within available resources produce the best solutions for the largest number of voters. The recent proposal of a 'cap' on the amount any person will have to spend on their social care in old age has the double effect of alleviating the fear of those who have anxiety about their future in old age and enabling the generation in middle age to know that their hope of receiving the major part of their inheritance will not be jeopardised if their parents become ill. Commending this proposal as meaning that 'nobody will have to sell their home so as to provide for their care' achieves a wide measure of political support as a result.

It is no criticism of politicians to point out that while their solutions offer a measure of satisfaction to different groups of voters they do so at the cost of accepting the transformations which money as it has become has brought about: houses have been transformed into a means to wealth and an insurance policy against the uncertainties of the future. We know that in accepting these transformations we are also accepting money's power over the aspirations and the fears of human beings. We also know that such acceptance of the transformative power of money has led, and will continue to lead, to a continual widening of the gap between rich and poor.[1] We also see those who need a home (as against an investment) finding it more and more difficult to afford one; and we know also that the housing market is operating in such a way as to increase the separation between regions of high prices and regions of low prices, a trend which the annual growth in house prices illustrates all too clearly with the enormous percentage price rises in London and its environs. Allowing money to exercise that level of control over the basic need human beings have for housing produces just such undesirable results, and the failure to grasp what is at the root of these undesirable outcomes simply means that they will continue into the indefinite future.

The faces gazing into the estate agent's window and the variety of aspirations and hopes which they represent show how it is that money has come to have the capacities of the idols we considered in the last chapter and the capacity the idols have to transform human desires and play on human fears. Not surprisingly, our ancestors, in their decision to place their trust in the God of Israel as against the idols, were led to some very definite convictions about the use of land and its ownership. For if land is above all else a *gift*, something we neither earn nor deserve, then making it into an index of prosperity by producing price increases that put housing themselves way beyond the reach of those with no land and no home denies the very belief in divine creation that religious people claim to profess.

So the faces gazing into the window of the estate agent show something not that dissimilar to what could be seen in the queue for lottery tickets with which this book began. There too we noticed what happens when major social outcomes are made to depend on arbitrary and random activities such as a lottery: the poorest end up paying most for the causes which the lottery 'supports'. That should not surprise us, for it is the poor who have the greatest reason for opting into an activity which offers a tiny chance of massive winnings when what their life situation offers those who do not possess a house with a rising price tag is a reasonable perception that they have no chance at all of a significant change in their circumstances. Those who enjoy museums and theatres and are glad when ancient buildings are restored with the aid of donations from the Heritage Lottery Fund need to be aware that they are doing so at the expense of people who struggle for the basic necessities of life. The plaques that memorialise the 'generosity' of the Heritage Lottery Fund are a standing witness to what is actually an act of exploitation; so is the prevalence of homelessness alongside the constantly rising price of housing.

Those who enjoy the proceeds of the lottery or of rising house prices need to be aware of something else also, something touching more profoundly on what faith is about: rising house prices, like the lottery, are not small activities carried on in one department of life and with no effect on the rest. In fact they offer a powerful image of the kind of world into which money as it has become, like the religions of the ancient deities, has propelled us. It is a world that pretends to be free but in fact offers only chaotic outcomes, in which a vision of humanity as it is intended to be is sacrificed for the sake of the well-being of the better off. The glittering money prizes and the huge prices commanded by the most fashionable properties for sale represent a caricature of the purpose of living, an eschatology of the idols, in which huge winnings are taken by some while the essential offer the gospel makes, of well-being and healing for all, is cast aside.

In the process, something is being changed at the heart of what it is to be human. The idols of old and the deities they represented were credited with changing their worshippers so that they came to resemble that which they worshipped. That reality has to be faced: in the way those deities created, and then met, the desires of their worshippers and apparently saved them from the patient obedience which their covenant with God required, so money has come to be looked to for the same purpose.

Two revealing slogans

Two of the most beguiling slogans of this money era illustrate this point most clearly. In the first flush of enthusiasm for consumer debt the credit card sponsored by Access, the precursor of what is now Mastercard, was advertised with the slogan 'Access takes the waiting out of wanting'. The significance of that offer cannot be overstated: the prospective customer was being told in no uncertain terms that the age of saving up, of prudence, of prioritising purchases in the light of your available income – these and other forms of 'waiting' were now over. In the brave new world this 'free money' was offering, you could have what you wanted when you wanted it and not have to wait until you could afford it – let alone be subjected to the indignity of being interrogated about whether you could. The arrival in banks of large sums of money that needed to be found a profitable home, multiplied because the bank only needed to keep a fraction in reserve, meant that the virtues of patience and prudence came to seem very old-fashioned indeed. Individuals might display those virtues, but they would be swimming against the tide of changed social attitudes. They would

notice their friends and neighbours and the things they had been
able to purchase by letting Access – and other lenders – 'take the
waiting out of wanting'.

A second revealing slogan shows the capacity of money
to change our desires. The two crossed fingers, the logo of the
National Lottery, represent a powerful symbol of the belief that
life is a gamble. The slogan that goes with it is 'It could be you'.
This is a good slogan, which might, and in the past did, encourage
people to think about some offering of time they might make to
help the poor or undertake some valuable social project. A story
would be told of some valuable piece of work, a life transformed,
a major project undertaken, a sacrifice made of time and ambition
for no tangible reward. Then the punch line: it could be you. It is
the slogan of vocation, four words that make a call, perhaps even
we might say a divine call, to do something you might not have
thought of doing, something you had imagined only claimed other
people.

But put the two crossed fingers logo alongside that slogan and
the meaning is quite different. What 'could be you' now is the status
of multi-millionaire; the right numbers that would win that night
might be yours; somebody is going to have their life transformed
– and 'it could be you'. The attitude suggested by the possibility of
this reward derives much of its power from the portrayal of those
with massive pay or bonuses, enjoying a lifestyle that is way beyond
the imagining of most who set off for work in the morning and
bring home an ordinary day's wage. But now, thanks to the lottery,
'it could be you'. It is money that might produce for you the major
life transformation you seek – not something so unrewarding as a
call to service.

An idol moulds our desiring

To make the claim that money has acquired the nature of an idol
is to recognise its capacity, in the quantity and volatility it now
exhibits, to change the desires of individuals and indeed whole
societies so that they 'become like what they worship', as oriented
towards measuring success by quantity and speed as the money they

are handling. So as money has increased in its quantity and volatility it has more and more acquired the capacity, as the idols of old did, to transform human desires. It was that recognition that led the Doctrine Commission of the Church of England, when it sought to produce its report on Christian anthropology, the understanding of what it is to be human, to decide that it was necessary to include, in a way that earlier generations might not have done, an account of money and its effects.

The Commission had chosen, perhaps unusually for an enterprise in Christian anthropology, to place at the centre of its work four aspects of human living – power, money, sex and time – where it judged the tradition of Christian wisdom, grounded in Scripture, would contribute much to the estimation of what *Being Human* (the title of the report) involved, and therefore to the promotion of human flourishing. Though the method was unusual, the inclusion of three of the topics – power, sex and time – might be thought fairly obvious in an account of human being. However, the tone as well as the content of the chapter on money reveals a Commission somewhat concerned lest its choice of that topic might strike the reader as eccentric and even inappropriate: after all, the Commission says,

> Money might not seem to be an essential and defining aspect of human nature. We know after all that there have been societies, groups and individuals who have lived without money, and that some such societies still exist; they are certainly no less human. Money seems more an accidental feature of developed human society, not an essential aspect of human nature or of our relationship to God.[2]

The decade since the report has seen a good deal of interest in the topic of money, its history and its nature, to the extent that the widespread assumption that we all know what money is, how it works and how it came to be what it now is has been shown to be a very unwise one. It is not just that, as the Commission observes: at this point in human cultural and social development, money is almost universal, and necessarily so. It cannot be avoided. We are obliged to be involved with money, simply in order to transact our lives. Life, in all its abundant possibilities, is unthinkable – more importantly, unliveable – without it. In a complex society such as ours, it is simply not possible to pursue self-sufficiency to the point where one never becomes involved with money.[3]

In particular, the Commission refers to the changes which recent decades have brought about, those described in Chapter 2, namely that through a combination of forces money is vastly more significant as a feature of our personal and social lives than used to be the case. Having accepted the account of money's recent history that has been given earlier, namely that money has expanded vastly in quantity through a combination of events – the massive increase in the price of oil meant that large sums found their way into the banking system; the fractional reserve system of banking allows banks to lend large multiples of the deposits they hold – and the huge advances in information technology which mean that money circulates not in the time it takes to transport notes and coins but in the microseconds it takes for computerised transactions to transfer money – the Commission contends that in that context it is hard to argue with the proposition that money has come to play a vastly increased part in the lives of individuals and societies. That is confirmed, for instance, by the existence in our weekend newspapers of sections with news of money, and advertisements designed to encourage you to make your money be more productive. This is quite clear evidence that even if humans are reluctant to note that ever increasing role played by money in their lives, the count of trees demolished to make way for that ever increasing volume of newsprint shows it all too clearly.

What this leads the Commission to say is that we would be wise not to accept too readily the widespread assumption that there is a substance called money about which we are free as human persons to take whatever attitude we may choose. It is too easy and convenient to accept that quoting 1 Timothy 6.10 – 'The love of money is a root of all kinds of evil' – confirms the happy thought that it is the *love of money* rather than money itself that is morally problematic. The Commission asks the question whether money itself as it has now become has effects that have moral consequences. Their conclusion is that when money grows exponentially in amount and speed of circulation it is also bound to grow in its capacity to be the source of changes in our pattern of desires: it carries the love of itself in its train. As we have already mentioned, among the most sinister ways in which this now very powerful medium alters human desires – though not the only one – is through its funding of advertising and the continuous presentation by press and broadcasting media of the view that it is by emulating the desires of the moneyed that the poor will find relief from their poverty: thus is the fundamental equality which is the presupposition of democracy effectively subverted. The right to vote is no protection against the power of wealth if money has itself become the means to persuade the voter that in the power of the wealthy lies their only key to a reasonable standard of life.

Yet even without the advertising of what money can buy, the mere fact that we are more and more preoccupied with money in our everyday dealings is ground enough for believing that money, so far from being a neutral substance, has the capacity to mould the human spirit. As the Commission says:

> This belief in our inner freedom to mould our own desires about money, tempting though it is, is also challenged in our own experience. Can anyone believe that the increased availability of credit does not at the same time change our moral sense about whether it is good or bad to be in debt? Does not the frequency with which we see huge prizes awarded as the random outcome of a gamble and huge rewards given to those at the head of organisations (even failing ones) affect how far money starts to glitter before us, enticing us with its capacity to procure what we want and calm our fears of finding ourselves destitute and in need? These are rhetorical questions: the evidence of those we know, let alone the evidence of research into such topics as student indebtedness, gives a very clear answer: the human will is shaped by that with which human beings occupy themselves every day and the assumptions they find themselves making.[4]

The frequency with which we handle money, talk about it, concern ourselves with it, all give it power over our lives. Money has numbers on it, and the numbers are decisive for many of our activities, purchases and choices. Nobody should assume that this does not dull our consciences, corporately and individually, so that ethical decisions which by their nature are complex, nuanced and spiritual become financial calculations. What has to be grasped, especially by people of faith, is that our ethical convictions only shape our behaviour after repeated patterns of behaviour – in this case about money – have shaped our consciences.

So for instance in their research into student debt, Emma Davies and Stephen Lea show quite clearly how student attitudes to going into debt were changed by their need to do so.

> Although [students] were not at first in favour of debt, to sustain an acceptable lifestyle, they found they had to go into debt. Once they had incurred debt, their attitude to debt changed, so that they became more tolerant. It would be interesting to know what happens to these individuals when they leave university. Will they take a more tolerant attitude to debt with them ... or will they take the opportunity to pay off student debts and, once free of debt, revert to a more typical anti-debt attitude?[5]

That research was undertaken in the early 1990s, and I encountered it in my research on debt. We know very well what has happened to that generation of students, and what is expected of their successors. For indebtedness is not simply necessary to 'sustain an acceptable lifestyle' but has, in the period since that research, become a necessity for any person wishing to receive a higher education.

That is not all we have learned about the capacity of our behaviour to shape our consciences: housing indebtedness (a possibly more accurate phrase than the more benign-sounding 'home ownership') is also a virtual necessity for having a home, and is part of the process by which, as we pointed out earlier, the bricks and mortar of our houses have moved from being simply our home to being our principal financial investment, and housing debt has become a virtuous condition in which to be.

There are of course individuals whose attitudes to money have not been changed by our daily experience of what money has now become; but the fact remains that what has happened to us as a society is a substantial alteration of the way money behaves and the way we behave with it. It has in effect come to be a divinity, taking control not just of our behaviour but also, as we shall see, of our values and our inner landscape.

Values by numbers – an idol's substitute ethics

What has happened to money is not to be identified with the activities of the greedy or of corporations with a sole concern to make larger profits. The problem – what makes Mammon an idol – is the infection of human beings' *best* intentions with the values system which money engenders. In 2011 I had occasion to reflect, five years on, on an event that played an enormous part in my thinking, but far more importantly had a dramatic effect on numerous people's lives, on the relations between the churches in South London and their local communities. The story was of the sale of the Octavia Hill estates by the Church Commissioners, not to another social housing agency but to the highest bidder. The result, five years on from the sale, was the final loss of all those properties to the social market; they are now entirely part of the grossly inflated London private housing market, unaffordable to local people, and disrupting the congregational life of local parishes. They are now subject to all the pressures that money has exerted on housing; the protection of those estates from those pressures was one of the achievements of Octavia Hill as the remarkable housing manager of the Church Commissioners a century before. The event has stayed with me not because of a wish to dissociate myself from the colleagues who voted, against a dissenting minority, to sell to the highest bidder; they were entirely honourable people acting, as they genuinely believed, in the Church's best interests. That I disagreed with them at the time is not the point. Rather, what the story demonstrates is that in a world dominated by money it will be precisely the *best* aims and intentions that will be subverted, and the Church Commissioners are far from being the only charitable organisation led into prioritising money over the less immediate objects of their charitable work. But the episode shows only too clearly where we have arrived. As the final loss of the housing to the social market happened, I wrote:

> As I write this, a group from [some] South London parishes are scheduled to deposit ash at Church House, Westminster, on the Tuesday of Holy Week. They are making this protest as a call to repentance to the Church Commissioners for the decision [five years ago] to sell the Octavia Hill Estates to the highest bidder rather than their being retained as the social housing that Octavia Hill had envisaged ...
>
> For those of us who were around at the time of the decision, the memory of that lost vote remains searing ... The perversity of the argument used at the time – that this [sale to the highest bidder] was necessary 'to support the mission of the Church' – is finally clear, if it was ever in doubt, now that the estates are all to be privately owned. They are now part of the market that raises prices to a level that local people can no longer afford.
>
> Communities, PCCs, the diocese of Southwark, archdeacons, area bishops, the Bishop of Southwark, and the Archbishop of Canterbury at the time could all see the damage that this sale to the highest bidder would do – precisely to 'the mission of the Church'.
>
> Only devotees of the power of money to cover all disasters could imagine that realising a few extra millions into the coffers of the Church Commissioners could make up for that damage. We all now know that selling the estates to the highest bidder, with no protection for the social-housing vision, would inflict a wound on the Church's mission which

will pass into the folklore of the parishes where the estates are located.

This story reveals exactly where we have got to in our attitude to money. Octavia Hill and the Church Commissioners of her day were not at all unaware of their duty to realise a return on their assets. The difference between them and those who took the decision to sell the estates to the highest bidder is that Hill and her contemporaries had a theology of 'enough'. For her, it was enough if the Commissioners realised five per cent on their assets, and her vision was of providing housing for local people within that discipline.

The 'highest bidder' mantra is exactly the opposite: enough is never enough. If you can get more, you must. And that is precisely the attitude – the religion of money – that brought the world financial system to the edge of collapse, and that remains unchallenged in too many circles today.

What stands in the way of serious reform of the financial system – a reform that, as the Christian Council for Monetary Justice (www.ccmj.org) constantly reminds us, requires that the production of money should not be in the hands of the banks who profit from it – is the fact that those with power have no theology of enough.

They will never have enough, and, by their commitment to constant growth, they will promote more and more crises, from financial collapse to resource depletion and climate change. And enough, as Bishop John V. Taylor said all those years ago, is enough.

The building in which the decision to sell the estates was taken was itself sold on to the House of Lords, and so church people will no longer pass the memorial plaque to Octavia Hill. But the story of her vision, and of what has happened to it in our time, had better be remembered for all it has to teach us about what happens when the power of money overreaches itself.

It is a danger from which the Church is not immune, as we can see. Only if that is learned and taken to heart will this sad story bear fruit in a better outcome.

On the morning of the day when the Assets Committee of the Church Commissioners would meet for what I sensed would be the final, and disastrous, decision effectively to sell the estates into the private market, I was allowed to join, and be supported by, members of the congregation at a eucharist at St Anne's, South Lambeth. As things have turned out, during this week I shall remember that event as, in a sense, Octavia Hill's last supper.[6]

The attractiveness of the idols and of the deities they represented, by comparison with the demanding austerity of the God of Israel, lay principally in their *immediacy* and their *visibility*. As we described them in Chapter 5, those two qualities gave them, from the point of view of a nation living out a fragile existence surrounded by hostile enemies, a very strong claim.

It is because it possesses a similar, and equally attractive, feature that money functions as an idol in the circumstances in which we now find ourselves. As well as having the influence it has in our lives because of the sheer quantity there is of it and the speed with which it can be deployed, it has that great virtue of immediacy and visibility. This is because, to state the obvious, money is denominated in *numbers*. As an index of relative value, therefore, it appears to offer a route to decision-making about the relative merit of different products or courses of action which is simple, clear and objective, without the subtlety and complexity of other forms of value. As the Chair of a local education committee was recorded as saying at the beginning of his Speech Day address, 'I can't tell you whether you're the best school in the borough, but I do know you're the cheapest.' Clearly, with whatever degree of irony, this was a speaker whose words bore the mark of Oscar Wilde's sharp contrast:

> *Lord Darlington*: What cynics you fellows are!
> *Cecil Graham*: What is a cynic? [*sitting on the back of the sofa*]
> *Lord Darlington*: A man who knows the price of everything and the value of nothing.
> *Cecil Graham*: And a sentimentalist, my dear Darlington, is a man who sees an absurd value in everything, and doesn't know the market price of any single thing.[7]

We know too that when decisions were made to change the way in which residential care was provided a substantial outsourcing of a number of necessary activities took place: the purpose was to save money. It is a process that continues now in the context of the need to reduce the levels of public debt. But that objective, an essentially financial one, has taken precedence over a number of other values which were sustained by the fact that those undertaking quite menial activities in residential homes were nonetheless part of the total team of providers. The point here is not that outsourcing was always wrong, but that the values of teamwork and solidarity stood no chance against the overriding pressure to achieve financial targets. We are not talking, that is to say, about a set of advantages and disadvantages which might be assessed equally in relation to a particular decision, but essentially responding to a situation in which one value, that with numbers on it, monetary value, would always predominate because of the power money had come to acquire.

That power presents itself as the most objective possible: what could be more objective than numbers? But in fact what the numbers stand for is a world view every bit as potent as that possessed by the cults of the ancient world and the deities they served. The numbers themselves may be capable of manipulation mathematically; but the reduction of values to numbers is the expression of a world view, the development of money into Mammon, of an instrument into an idol.

But in the Doctrine Commission's comment reported above – 'Does not the frequency with which we see huge prizes awarded as the random outcome of a gamble and huge rewards given to those at the head of organisations (even failing ones) affect how far money starts to glitter before us, enticing us with its capacity to procure what we want and calm our fears of finding ourselves destitute and in need?' – our attention is drawn not just to the mutation of values into money with numbers, but other significant changes to our inner world: the form which money has taken and the power which it has come to exercise through its growth in quantity and speed of transmission exercises a far from benign influence on some of the most important aspirations we have for the development of the human spirit.

After all, if money presents itself as a *god*, is it not bound to have a *spirituality*, a *prayer life* which it enjoins upon its worshippers/followers/devotees? Does it have *rituals*, *acts of worship*, *festivals* as the God whom Christians worship also has, and how are they different?

Certainly it seems to have its equivalent of 'saints'; the heroes of the money world are not hard to find: they are well rewarded, with a lifestyle reflecting their successful following of the 'discipleship' money commends. Money has its festivals too: the grand sale, when money gives you more than at other times, when shop windows are ablaze with news of *price* overwhelming any news of the quality, utility and design of the goods, in a great festival of 'buy because it's cheaper', not 'buy because it's good/beautiful/fit for purpose'.

If money has acquired an array of 'saints', 'festivals' and 'rituals', what kind of *discipleship* does it enjoin upon us? If the virtues of prudence and discretion which once were required of us in our dealings with money have been replaced by an exalted sense of the possibilities of manipulation and the virtue of ostentatious wealth, we must expect that the 'prayer life' required in the service of money also has its own distinct characteristics: our daily bread is the news of the value of our house, our bonds, our equities – if we have them. The reality of the lives of those who do not have money is not allowed to detain us long, let alone influence our decisions, lest they disturb us in the task of contemplating what money has to offer by reminding us of the penalties of exclusion from the money-kingdom. This is a god with disciples, with a prayer life, with every capacity to take hold of and direct the human spirit in ways of which we need to be aware.

Quantity, volatility and noise

To take one of the most pressing examples of this effect on the spirit, there are important and widely accepted reasons, at least in theory if not in practice, why silence should be highly valued as a key aspect of the life of the human spirit. While discovering the quality of stillness or prayerful contemplation in the context of numerous interior and exterior distractions has always presented difficulties for the person of faith, and while wealth has always been the occasion of covetousness, ambition and hyper-activity, I suggest that there are particular obstacles to stillness and recollectedness which are brought about by the developments in the creation and manipulation of money as they have been described in this book. Given the psalmist's comment, to which reference has already been made – 'Those who make them become like them, and so do those who trust in them' – these obstacles to stillness can best be described under the three headings of quantity, volatility and noise.

Quantity
There is, for the reasons I have given, much more money about, and the *effective* quantity is even more enlarged by the technology that speeds up its circulation. I have described some of the ways in which that has changed our values and our desires. Money has co-opted us not just into a world of numbers but as a result into a world where quantity is apt to be the most important consideration. As is to be expected from the way an idol inserts its values into all parts of our life, the fact that money is measured by numbers not only affects our approach to money itself, but conditions all planning and decision-making by the way in which it privileges a quantitative measure of worth and outcomes.

So, for all the lip service that is paid to the idea that 'growth' involves many aspects and not just measurable size and quantity, there is an irresistible tendency for that to be the driving concern in all that we do. So, for example, in church life members do not usually express openly the idea that numbers of worshippers or the income they provide should be the measure of the 'success' of a church; but even where numbers and size are not mentioned it is not hard to see how those become the dominant concerns. All will agree that there is such a thing as growth in faith, growth in the spiritual life, growth in understanding and growth in commitment to the life of the local community, but the numerical measures which are characteristic of monetary evaluation intrude themselves as primary. Mention 'church growth' and everybody knows you are about to present strategic proposals for increasing the number of people who attend.

This phenomenon is no more nor less than churches' co-option into the pattern of valuation which money and its power press upon us. In all the agonising there has been in public and in private about the crisis of 2008 and what was to be done in the years following, restoring 'growth' has been the spoken and unspoken objective. The political debate has been about how individuals' and families' standard of living that has been 'reduced' could be 'restored' to what it was before the crisis: that such should be the aim is not questioned. That we might need to be content with less, that we might need to learn ways of creative living that do not depend on growing resources, that those who have chosen poverty might have learned a wisdom from which we could all learn – these questions are enormously difficult to raise; what determines the priorities we have for our politicians, over and above all others, is not that they fulfil the traditional tasks of government, the maintenance of peace and order and the defence of the realm, but that they find ways to increase the *quantitative* measures of our society, and in particular the gross national product.

We know that there are ways of promoting a sense of human fulfilment and of asking the kinds of questions which will yield insight into whether people feel fulfilled; we will say, and mean, that 'money isn't everything', but the power of its quantitative and measurable energy overwhelms us when we come to make the choices that are important. Among the more revealing aspects of our real belief system is what we find it necessary to be secretive about. Even in the context of relationships of honesty and openness, in which all sorts of feelings can be revealed in confidence, why is money a topic surrounded by silence and secrecy? The answer lies, as we have seen is the case with idols, in the apparent precision with which we can make financial valuations because money has numbers on it.

You enter a large house, and the next day a much smaller one. You will have an impression of size, and perhaps of the difference in wealth of the owners of the two properties. But you will know that there are factors you would need to be aware of if you were to form a reliable conclusion of the relative wealth in money of the two property owners. A fashionable studio flat in a very prestigious part of the capital city will be much smaller than a rambling farmhouse in the depth of the countryside; but you will not immediately know which is worth more. One property may have serious structural faults; another might house a significant artistic collection. In many situations you may be able to form an impression of wealth or poverty; what you will not be able to do is make an instant calculation that will tell you the relative wealth of two people.

Money is different. You add up the numbers, subtract the larger from the smaller and, provided you have the information, the relativities are clear. The numerical character of money, combined with the massive expansion in the amount of it, creates a situation where a pause for reflection, a weighing of different factors, qualitative questions in general, are pushed into the background against the sheer attractiveness of being able to answer questions by counting numbers. Less and less a discipline, monetary considerations become a scale of value in themselves as quantitative thinking overshadows the qualitative; in planning an academic syllabus or designing a course, money has moved from being a limiting factor to being a major driving force in the discussion. In such an environment calculation becomes more significant than contemplation, the mind's active processes more than its receptive ones. It is not that a concern with money is something that has never been around before; only that its quantity and speed have made it a pervasive and overwhelming feature of human thinking, and therefore significantly enhanced its capacity to alter the patterns of human desiring. And as money changes the pattern of desiring, it also spreads its influence into our patterns of thinking, leading to the need to calculate the *cost* of any time spent in simple receiving. And since in such a world 'time is money', we notice the second feature of money to mould the pattern of human thinking and feeling, namely its capacity to speed up our processes at, we might say, 'all costs'.

Volatility

The technology that means that money can be processed and transmitted in microseconds is naturally available to us in many aspects of our life, and communication has been altered dramatically by the electronic wizardry that means that a question can be asked and answered across thousands of miles in next to no time. Yet at the same time we know that stillness and rest is a significant requirement for the living of a wholesome and healthy life. For all the advantages we gain, therefore, from the speed with which it is possible to communicate, conversations abound in which people grumble about the drivenness of the email culture, and that what is in principle an opportunity to enhance our administration and nourish our friendships has created a situation where the over-full inbox constitutes, as well as a standing rebuke and a further chore, a barrier to the taking of adequate time to reflect on what needs to be said or done in response to a message received.

The connection of this with the ubiquitous power of money lies in the drive that money has to be making more of itself. When machinery that involves large capital expenditure is idle it represents a problem of inefficiency which management needs to take very seriously. But it is a further step – part of the idolising of money and the extension of its power – that money itself must not be allowed to be idle; so a major part of the financial sector's concern is to ensure that money is moved quickly to where it will gain more of itself. The criticism of the financial sector that it is prone to short-term thinking is often fair: what needs to be realised, however, is that that short-term thinking derives from the emergence of money as that which determines the speed at which things need to be done.

When people are paid a piece-work rate it is true to say that 'time is money'; that is what it costs in human labour to make something or perform a service, that is to say to provide something in the real economy. What we notice when money extends its influence in the manner of an idol is its capacity to give priority to speed of return. Money has prioritised speed over other qualities. So it is not for nothing that money is referred to as a 'liquid asset', its value realisable in an instant. Money is justified by its capacity to produce more of itself, and unlike the obligations imposed by ownership of other kinds of wealth – to keep the outside of your house painted so that the window frames don't rot or to have your car serviced so that it remains roadworthy – money must not remain idle, but ways and means must be found to keep it 'active', and for money to be 'active' it must be making more of itself. In a world of instant, computer-driven financial trading, no second must be lost: money must not lie idle in an account that produces no income, must be kept 'active' at all times. The working hours of people in the financial sector, needing to keep awake and at their desks across time zones, bear witness to a virtual world in which money and its requirement to be active, making more of itself, drives the pattern of human activity before it; and stillness and even leisure are evaluated in terms of their expense – and money's time is money. And money's reward for this hyperactivity? More of itself.

The events of 2008 onwards present an apocalyptic vision of volatility: money and the capacity to make more of itself became a principal, highly rewarded, way of using the human intellect, driving the invention of more and more ingenious ways of making money make money, and making it quickly. Volatility was not seen – until it was too late – to spell a lack of prudence, an overheating of driven minds: rather, the quickest thinkers gained the highest rewards, in a world increasingly frantic, and in a linguistic environment in which the language of numbers shouted at high speed or displayed on flickering screens becomes the dominant noise, drowning out all restful stillness. For money is impatient of a quiet world; volatility is its nature, and such are the patterns of behaviour honoured in a world in which money's influence predominates. It is its own reward, and forms its devotees to be as volatile as it is itself, for we become like what we worship, in this case restless and driven creatures, no longer controlling the instrument of valuation and exchange but allowing it in its driving pursuit of itself to control us. Nor are quantity and speed the only characteristics of the world of money's creation: in its quest for more and in the speed with which its ambition needs to be satisfied, it is also the enemy of stillness.

Noise

For none of money's characteristics minister much to the quest for stillness and reflection, let alone to the quest for silence, only to an increasingly frantic and noisy environment. In part that is literally true: 'noise pollution' is an increasing phenomenon, and not just for those who live under airport flight paths or near to motorways with their constant flow of high-speed traffic, or in town centres which are not allowed a time of rest from the needs of consumers.

There is, however, a different kind of noise also with which to contend, the noise we refer to when we speak of the 'signal to noise ratio', the power of the money culture to engage in systematic distraction, the obscuring of the 'signal' of what actually requires our attention. In our relating of this phenomenon to the accounts we have of idolatry, money as idol talks the language of disturbance, an obstruction to the clear 'signal' of divine utterance. The reason the idols are said to 'make no sound in their throats' is that they contrast with the clarity of the divine demand, and they generate confusion of utterance and thought. In our society money does this not just for those professionally involved with money, the bankers and the brokers, but for the society at large where the 'voice' of money is a constant source of distraction requiring attention to itself, and therefore to the world it is making, away from the possibilities of contemplation and attentiveness. Its exponential growth, its acceleration and its constant need to attend to itself become models for our interaction with the world around us. The imprudence and the near disaster that stared us in the face in the recent crisis, and continues to do so, are direct results of that. As the psalmist puts it most graphically in a description of what happens when the world is submitted to the chaos such divinities engender,

> They have neither knowledge nor understanding,
>   they walk around in darkness;
>   all the foundations of the earth are shaken.

(Psalm 82.5)

What kind of economy is it that submits us to an increase of quantitative thinking, volatility and distraction? It is Mammon's economy, and we need to take a closer look at the nature of that economy if we are to consider whether there might be an alternative.

Notes

[1] For the destructive effects of widening inequality, see most famously Richard Wilkinson and Kate Pickett, *The Spirit Level* (Penguin, 2009). The French economist Thomas Piketty has persuasively maintained that there is a 'natural' tendency towards the widening of that gap. See his *Capital in the Twenty-First Century* (Belknap, 2014); cf. review by Thomas Edsall, *New York Times*, January 2014.

[2] Doctrine Commission of the Church of England, *Being Human* (Church House Publishing, 2003), p. 55.

[3] *Being Human*, p. 55.

[4] *Being Human*, p. 68.

[5] Emma Davies and Stephen E. G. Lea, 'Student Attitudes to Student Debt', *Journal of Economic Psychology* 16 (1995), p. 678.

[6] Peter Selby, 'Lament at Octavia Hill's last supper', *Church Times*, 19 April 2011.

[7] Oscar Wilde, *Lady Windermere's Fan* (1892), Act III. For the host of literary references that illustrate ambivalence towards money, see Kevin Jackson (ed.), *The Oxford Book of Money* (Oxford University Press, 1996).

7

Mammon's economy portrayed

We have seen what has happened to our money, and after examining the characteristics of idols and the deities which they represented in the ancient world have seen how the behaviour of money as it has become replicates many of those characteristics. In particular the political and personal outcomes of the behaviour of money unmasks it as a contemporary idol. The parallels that have been drawn derive from debates and indeed conflicts within the Hebrew people, as they have been recorded in their history and in the psalms from which we have quoted.

There is a stark contrast to be drawn between the belief system that involved seeing life as the outcome of the chaotic results of conflicts among the deities, being formed as individuals and societies to be like them, living by the values they represent, offering the sacrifices they demand and acting out the oppression of the poor and vulnerable, on the one hand, and trust in the covenant God who requires justice, mercy and an appropriately humble walking in his way.

The shaking of the foundations of the earth emerges as not too much of an exaggeration of the consequences of making the wrong choice between God and Mammon. As we contemplate the serious effects of resource depletion and climate change, most devastatingly for the poorest nations and individuals, as well of course as for the remarkably diverse population of animals and plants with whom human beings share this planet and without whom they would not survive, the language and rituals of a heaven populated by deities in conflict and an earth populated by the idols made to represent them lose some of their remoteness. We find that humankind in this generation is faced with some remarkably similar challenges: to submit to the world formed by money as it has become or to take seriously the inevitable results of doing so and the contemporary opportunities of a return to the ways of justice and mercy.

It turns out that in the renewing of the divine covenant to which the Gospels bear witness we find some very powerful and nuanced accounts of what those choices amount to. In the chapter on 'Forgotten Wisdom' in my previous book, *Grace and Mortgage*, I refer to that ancient wisdom principally in relation to the matter of debt and usury. But the economic wisdom reaffirmed in the Gospels extends more widely than that into the whole realm of the economics of Mammon and the economic implications of the imminence of the Kingdom of God. I propose to illustrate this with reference to four of the parables of Jesus.

The parables: a history of preaching

The long history of scholarship about the parables has caused many earlier assumptions to be re-examined, and has to some extent rehabilitated some of the varieties of interpretation that have appeared at different points in the history of preaching. However, two preliminary points need to be made before the parable discussions that follow, because in the variety of settings in which I have discussed these matters with various audiences it has become clear that there is some need for our minds to be liberated from two particular ways in which the parables have been understood and taught, and which obscure some of the richness which they have the capacity to convey.

The first of these features of the preaching of the parables is the tendency to make the assumption that because the parables are parables of the Kingdom which seek to describe the character of that Kingdom this means that the financial aspects of the stories are somehow incidental to a more spiritual and general moral meaning. It is not at all uncommon for a person introducing a parable to seek to disabuse the hearers of any notion that the parable connects with the details of the economy to which we are accustomed. So exposition of the parable of the labourers in the vineyard – to which we shall be returning as one of our examples – is quite commonly introduced with the observation that 'this is of course not a story about how to run a vineyard'. The 'of course' that often appears here is quite revealing, implying as it does that Jesus would not have concerned himself with a matter so technical and mundane that would nowadays be the subject of detailed consideration in the Human Resources department of the company. The parable then becomes a somewhat general commendation of divine generosity, contrasted naturally enough with the lack of generosity exhibited by the workers hired at the beginning of the working day, a lack of generosity also understood in the most general of terms. In that generalising, the specificity of their grievance is lost.

It is a further implication of this 'generalising' of the 'message' of the parables that generosity is a *general* quality of God's dealings with the world, and that any suggestion that the financial aspects of the parable need specific attention means that the story will be 'reduced' to 'mere economics'. It is in fact the reduction of the parable to a general moral tale that has to be guarded against.

With this teaching of the parables as general moral tales goes the second tendency which needs a careful critique. If the parables become general moral tales, the characters in them are likely to be divided between 'good' and 'bad', those who behave in the right way and those who do not; in particular, in parables with a 'boss' figure, for example the owner of the vineyard or the rich man who goes on a journey, that person is apt to be regarded as the principal exemplar of moral behaviour, and to be assumed to 'stand for' God in the story. This resembles the interpretation, frequently heard, that assumes that when God speaks in the concluding chapters of the book of Job we are hearing the voice of God as the author has come to understand God – an assumption that is very puzzling since in no way does 'God's' answer really address the writer's struggles with suffering, and the God who speaks leaves all the major theological questions about suffering open, as may well have been the writer's intention. So it is not to be assumed that there will be 'good' and 'bad' people in the parables or that the 'Lord' or 'King' or 'Owner' somehow stands for God.

In the following examinations of four 'economic' parables we may expect to see a highly realistic account of the world as it is, that is to say what a world is like when money rules it. The hearer is left to understand what kind of world would exist if the divine covenant were, as is promised, 'written on the hearts' of God's people, the determining formation of their lives. But before we can know what such a world would be like, taking seriously what the world actually is like is of the first importance.

Parable 1: 'You have made them equal to us'

'For the kingdom of heaven is like a landowner who went out early in the morning to hire labourers for his vineyard. After agreeing with the labourers for the usual daily wage, he sent them into his vineyard. When he went out about nine o'clock, he saw others standing idle in the market-place; and he said to them, "You also go into the vineyard, and I will pay you whatever is right." So they went. When he went out again about noon and about three o'clock, he did the same. And about five o'clock he went out and found others standing around; and he said to them, "Why are you standing here idle all day?" They said to him, "Because no one has hired us." He said to them, "You also go into the vineyard." When evening came, the owner of the vineyard said to his manager, "Call the labourers and give them their pay, beginning with the last and then going to the first." When those hired about five o'clock came, each of them received the usual daily wage. Now when the first came, they thought they would receive more; but each of them also received the usual daily wage. And when they received it, they grumbled against the landowner, saying, "These last worked only one hour, and you have made them equal to us who have borne the burden of the day and the scorching heat." But he replied to one of them, "Friend, I am doing you no wrong; did you not agree with me for the usual daily wage? Take what belongs to you and go; I choose to give to this last the same as I give to you. Am I not allowed

to do what I choose with what belongs to me? Or are you
envious because I am generous?" So the last will be first, and
the first will be last.'

(Matthew 20.1–16)

In the 'moral tale' version of this story, the landowner is likely to be
given a halo as an especially altruistic and generous person, living
out his conviction that people should be paid according to their
need rather than to the hours they have put in. The workers hired at
the beginning of the day, on the other hand, are usually presented as
mean and jealous, concerned to achieve the differential pay which
they see as their right for the extra work they have done. The only
criticism of the landowner is likely to be that if he did not expect
the reaction that came to his generosity that shows a certain naivety.

This very common exposition makes a number of assumptions:
we are told nothing of the original motivation of the landowner,
but we do learn something of his operating principles. First and
foremost he is clear that the vineyard is his and that he is free to do
with his wealth exactly what he chooses. His response to the workers
hired at the beginning of the day is in effect curmudgeonly and
authoritarian; he asserts that he is being generous, but his behaviour
towards those who have done a whole day's work is far from being
that; he simply asserts his ownership rights and insists on the letter
of the contract they entered into. On the other hand we are told
nothing about the amount of work the different groups of workers
achieved or whether that was relevant to the landowner's decision.

What are we told? We learn only that the characters in the
story behave entirely in accordance with what we might expect
of them in a world in which the morality of money is the one
that guides them. What it produces is a combination of high-
handedness and envy – again exactly as we would expect. We
learn how money rules, and if we understand that we can begin to
reflect on the different economy which the ministry and teaching
of Jesus is intended to inaugurate, and the reversals of behaviour
and outcomes that we are to expect ('The first shall be last and the
last first'). We can also expect what transpires in the narrative of
the gospel story: what happens to Jesus as a result of the teaching

he offers and the community he inaugurates is foreshadowed in the conflict we can see in the parable. An order in which equality is promoted provokes rage and defensiveness on the part of those with an investment in the current way of seeing the world. To witness our contemporary debate on welfare, characterised as it is by division – artificial or real – between those 'living a life on welfare' and 'hardworking families' is, in the light of this parable, not in the least surprising; but it is also to bring into that debate the question that the parable raises about the kind of response we might seek to make in the light of a different set of values, without being surprised by the reaction of the various characters who live in the world as it is: the responses described, the authoritarianism, the jealousy are only what we know would happen in the world we too inhabit. Sovereign power in the parable is exercised, we might reflect, by money.

Parable 2: 'Pay what you owe'

> Then Peter came and said to him, 'Lord, if another member of the church sins against me, how often should I forgive? As many as seven times?' Jesus said to him, 'Not seven times, but, I tell you, seventy-seven times.
>
> 'For this reason the kingdom of heaven may be compared to a king who wished to settle accounts with his slaves. When he began the reckoning, one who owed him ten thousand talents was brought to him; and, as he could not pay, his lord ordered him to be sold, together with his wife and children and all his possessions, and payment to be made. So the slave fell on his knees before him, saying, "Have patience with me, and I will pay you everything." And out of pity for him, the lord of that slave released him and forgave him the debt. But that same slave, as he went out, came upon one of his fellow-slaves who owed him a hundred denarii; and seizing him by the throat, he said, "Pay what you owe." Then his fellow-slave fell down and pleaded with him,

"Have patience with me, and I will pay you." But he refused; then he went and threw him into prison until he should pay the debt. When his fellow-slaves saw what had happened, they were greatly distressed, and they went and reported to their lord all that had taken place. Then his lord summoned him and said to him, "You wicked slave! I forgave you all that debt because you pleaded with me. Should you not have had mercy on your fellow-slave, as I had mercy on you?" And in anger his lord handed him over to be tortured until he should pay his entire debt. So my heavenly Father will also do to every one of you, if you do not forgive your brother or sister from your heart.'

(Matthew 18.21–35)

As in the last parable, we find 'stakeholder reaction' very prominent in this story, and given how audiences today react to the events we should not be surprised at what the reaction is, even if on this occasion the 'king' sides with the fellow slaves. We may imagine, therefore, that the audience which first heard the parable would likewise have reacted negatively to the actions of the slave who, having been bailed out himself, declines to offer the much smaller debt remission his colleague needs. Very readily, the moral conclusion is articulated: the king has been generous; the slave who had his debt remitted shows meanness.

But that leaves out of the account the basis of his reaction. The assumption is that a person who receives a bailout should be generous to any debtor he encounters, and become the same kind of generous creditor that his king showed himself to be. But how realistic is that 'moral' evaluation? Is it not rather the case that a person who has such a narrow escape would, in his relief, be determined to make absolutely sure that he did all he could not to land in such a situation again? Would not that be the far more likely reaction? Does not this story represent a very accurate account of the real world of Mammon – where its harshness (even when there is a temporary relief) is to be expected – and therefore the world of 'forgiveness' represents a far more 'counter-cultural' response than the moral outrage of the fellow slaves (and ourselves) suggests? A world in which bailout engenders generosity and further bailouts is a very different one from the one to which we are accustomed, and if we wish to look for confirmation that that is the case we have only to consider what were in fact the results of the bank bailouts of the years following 2008. For was not the expectation that if banks were bailed out they would be prepared to lend to the businesses which were seen as the key to economic recovery? And was not the actual experience exactly the opposite? The surprise of ministers that their messages encouraging banks to lend again was surely misplaced: were not the banks bound to respond to the events of the recent past out of a massive anxiety to make sure such things did not occur again and that they would put their own corporate interests first? And if those who expected recapitalised banks to support the economy had read this parable through realistic rather than moralistic spectacles might they have been rather less surprised?

And as to the reaction of the other slaves, we know how their reaction to a monetary bailout came to be reflected in their response to Jesus: they were happy enough that they should receive healing and even food when they needed it, but when it became clear that this was a policy, a way of being, which they were also to display, the response was entirely that of the bailed-out slave: 'away with him'.

For this is a story that invites the recognition of the contrast between the way of Mammon, so accurately described, and the contrasting road of generosity and forgiveness. Just how counter-cultural that is this story makes clear, and what it would cost to take a different way. What the story also makes clear is that as the story came to be recorded and repeated within the life of the earliest Christian community it was heard as a prophecy of what would happen to the world if it stayed with Mammon's way.

Parable 3: 'I knew you were a harsh man'

'For it is as if a man, going on a journey, summoned his slaves and entrusted his property to them; to one he gave five talents, to another two, to another one, to each according to his ability. Then he went away. The one who had received the five talents went off at once and traded with them, and made five more talents. In the same way, the one who had the two talents made two more talents. But the one who had received the one talent went off and dug a hole in the ground and hid his master's money. After a long time the master of those slaves came and settled accounts with them. Then the one who had received the five talents came forward, bringing five more talents, saying, "Master, you handed over to me five talents; see, I have made five more talents." His master said to him, "Well done, good and trustworthy slave; you have been trustworthy in a few things, I will put you in charge of many things; enter into the joy of your master." And the one with the two talents also came forward, saying, "Master, you handed over to me two talents; see, I have made two more talents." His master said to him, "Well done, good and trustworthy slave; you have been trustworthy in a few things, I will put you in charge of many things; enter into the joy of your master." Then the one who had received the one talent also came forward, saying, "Master, I knew that you were a harsh man, reaping where you did not sow, and gathering where you did not scatter seed; so I was afraid, and I went and hid your talent in the ground. Here you have what is yours." But his master replied, "You wicked and lazy slave! You knew, did you, that I reap where I did not sow, and gather where I did not scatter? Then you ought to have invested my money with the bankers, and on my return I would have received what was my own with interest. So take the talent from him, and give it to the one with the ten talents. For to all those who have, more will be given, and they will have an abundance; but from those who have nothing, even what they have will be taken away. As for this worthless slave, throw him into the outer darkness, where there will be weeping and gnashing of teeth.'"

(Matthew 25.14–30)

All three slaves understood very well what the expectations were of the enterprise in which their master was engaged, and indeed what kind of enterprise it was. The mission statement was about the making of money. And the characteristics of that activity are well understood: reaping where you have not sown and gathering where you have not scattered the seed are an accurate picture of what money has become in the frantic and disastrous world of the last few years. The point is that all three slaves and their master understood that equally well and agreed about it.

In every case it meant the master getting others to engage in making the money, and in the case of those to whom the largest sums were allocated the results were likely to be very gratifying. But what if you were a person allocated so little that you would never win? The risks of losing were far more significant if you had very little to start with, and fear of losing everything became the dominant driving thought behind the activities of the one who had very little. And when the accounts were added up he could at least say that he had not lost anything.

But that was not going to be a route that would satisfy the master, for whom the maximising of return was all-important. Why had he not invested the money with bankers, people who would pay interest from their own trading activities and offer an assured return: surely that would have been a disaster-proof way of reaping without sowing and gathering without scattering. Why had the slave with the least been so paralysed by fear as to do nothing with the money except the all-important achievement of keeping its value secure? Precisely because he had the most to lose – not the most in terms of the amount of money, but the most because he would have lost everything, unlike his colleagues who would only have lost a proportion of the money they used to trade. But the world of Mammon exacted its price anyway, and what he had was taken from him and given to the one most adept at conforming to the culture of the enterprise.

We are very familiar with expositions of this parable that focus on people being enterprising and using what they had to good effect, an exposition in justification of trade and enterprise. (The happy coincidence of the double meaning of 'talent' in English makes it possible to relate the parable to all the 'gifts' of the hearers.) But what such an exposition actually offers is a moral justification for 'reaping where you do not sow and gathering where you do not scatter'; it does not offer any critique of such a view of enterprise, one that paralyses with fear those who have least and eventually causes them to lose even what they have. Such an enterprise, the Mammon culture, engenders fear and, as we see here and have seen in the way in which the trading activity of the world works out, also results in the enhancement of inequality.

Released from seeing the parable as a moral tale justifying the Mammon-driven world as it is, we can see the critical judgement it makes on such a world, and the results of living uncritically in it. What release from such an exposition also does is remedy the fear-laden paralysis which will otherwise burden those who have least. Knowing that world as it is makes it possible to decide to live in a different one.

Parable 4: 'Take your bill and make it eighty'

Then Jesus said to the disciples, 'There was a rich man who had a manager, and charges were brought to him that this man was squandering his property. So he summoned him and said to him, "What is this that I hear about you? Give me an account of your management, because you cannot be my manager any longer." Then the manager said to himself, "What will I do, now that my master is taking the position away from me? I am not strong enough to dig, and I am ashamed to beg. I have decided what to do so that, when I am dismissed as manager, people may welcome me into their homes." So, summoning his master's debtors one by one, he asked the first, "How much do you owe my master?" He answered, "A hundred jugs of olive oil." He said to him, "Take your bill, sit down quickly, and make it fifty." Then he asked another, "And how much do you owe?" He replied, "A hundred containers of wheat." He said to him, "Take your bill and make it eighty." And his master commended the dishonest manager because he had acted shrewdly; for the children of this age are more shrewd in dealing with their own generation than are the children of light. And I tell you, make friends for yourselves by means of dishonest wealth[1] so that when it is gone, they may welcome you into the eternal homes.

'Whoever is faithful in a very little is faithful also in much; and whoever is dishonest in a very little is dishonest also in much. If then you have not been faithful with the dishonest wealth, who will entrust to you the true riches? And if you have not been faithful with what belongs to another, who will give you what is your own? No slave can serve two masters; for a slave will either hate the one and love the other, or be devoted to the one and despise the other. You cannot serve God and wealth.'[2]

(Luke 16.1–13)

The verses which follow this parable show that the understanding of it caused many generations of hearers, beginning with the first, great difficulties, and those verses are very clearly not directly related to the parable but rather are a selection of sayings which by their proximity to it might assist the reader in finding a meaning in the story. The difficulty is of course compounded if the expositor is committed to working out who is the 'good person' in the story, and even more if the manager's boss is somehow supposed to represent God, for in that case the behaviour being commended appears not to be very commendable.

However, what we have here, once again, is an exposé of the real Mammon-driven world as it is, the behaviour it expects and the conduct it is willing to reward. The manager is commended for achieving a quick resolution of the outstanding debts of his master; what he manages by the reduction of the two debts which are described is decidedly a win–win solution to the problem with which he is faced as he deals with his master's anger and his own future: the debtors win because they achieve a reduction in their liability; the master wins because the debt is apparently now an achievable sum for the debtors; and the manager wins because he has so ingratiated himself with the two debtors as to ensure that when his dismissal takes effect there will be those who are indebted to him. For his is a world where shrewdness is all, where it becomes the most important virtue, and for that the manager is commended, just as the slaves in parable 3 above are commended for their willingness to risk disaster in the interests of enabling their owner to reap where he had not sown. The earliest Christians found in the account of this manager's behaviour the possibility of living with wealth if they had it – a less stark choice than being required to give it all away – but fundamentally the account in the parable is of the world as it currently is. It is not, however, a condoning of that world, let alone a commendation of it, and once that is taken seriously we are not in the difficult position of finding the parable giving support to behaviour we would generally find undesirable.

The world of Mammon – and the possibility of another one

The economy (*oikonomia*) is as we observed at the outset of this exploration the law and custom of the household (the 'manager' in parable 4 above is an *oikonomos*, the person who regulates the household). The parables we have examined here are descriptions of what the household is like, and what its laws and customs will be, if it is regulated by Mammon. That description bears a remarkable resemblance to our description of the household we now inhabit as described in earlier chapters. We know that such a world creates its own morality and generates outcomes which are not just disadvantageous to the household but are showing the capacity to bring disaster upon it. At the very least we have shown the extent to which the crisis that we are passing through, and the even worse ones that await us if money-driven capitalism is allowed to continue as it currently is, parallels the world of the idols, and specifically of Mammon, as the biblical record portrays it.

Mammon's world is not, however, the only world the biblical record portrays. For what it seeks to set before its readers is the possibility of a transition to a different world, one in which the arbitrariness of Mammon's world is replaced by a way of life in which a destructive chaos is replaced by a benign order, in which the behaviours commended in Mammon's world are replaced by those which accord with both the gospel and what it will take to secure a future for the planet, for the species which inhabit it and for humankind which, according to the biblical record, has been entrusted with its guardianship. In such a world we shall walk where our ancestors walked along the path of trust and faithfulness, grounded in a secure conviction about how the world is meant to be.

It is still the law and custom of the household, but it is a household living in safety and justice together.

Notes

1 The words translated 'dishonest wealth' are in the original 'the Mammon of unrighteousness/injustice'. Mammon, a transliterated Aramaic word, is used in preference to the Greek equivalent, and in this form is made to look very like the name of a deity, for example 'the Baal of Peor'. For the variety of interpretations of the parable and the difficulty to which that continuing debate bears witness, see commentaries on St Luke's Gospel, for example C. F. Evans, *St Luke* (SCM Press, 1990), pp. 594–603.

2 The word translated 'wealth' is in the original 'Mammon'. See note 1 above.

8

A merciful economy[1]

Letting things count without our counting them

Do you promote recession when you weed your garden? After all, you don't need to: you can ring someone advertising their services as a gardener, and pay them to pull up the weeds. If you do that then you and the gardener would have contributed to the economic growth which is eluding our politicians. If you pull the weeds up yourself, you don't. The prospective gardener with his card in the local shop window wouldn't earn what you have to pay him and the national economic cake won't expand at all. The strange thing is, it won't make much difference to the state of the garden: provided you can tell a plant from a weed and go to it with energy the weed-free patch will be just as free of weeds whether the person who pulled them up got paid for doing so or not. It's just that the actual output – a garden without weeds – isn't what counts; only money counts. If of course you don't hire a gardener you can spend the money in some other way that contributes to the GDP – or keep it in the bank where perhaps they will lend it to someone who will invest it or spend it, perhaps contributing to the GDP. But then the gardener, if you pay him to pull up the weeds, might spend what you pay him on something else – so that it makes yet a further contribution to the GDP. As we have been noticing, it is money that has the numbers on it, and so it is money moving around that counts, and if you don't pay a gardener that bit of money doesn't move around, and so doesn't count.

That's the justification of the bonus culture, of course. Here are people doing things that actually *count*, and so they should be rewarded in a way that counts – and that means, since we know no better way, in *money*.

If good outcomes – a weed-free garden or for that matter home-cooked food – don't count, there's also the fact that some bad outcomes do count. You buy fuel for the car; you drive the car; you emit exhaust fumes; you increase the carbon dioxide in the atmosphere. But the fuel, the maintenance of the roads, the wages of the mechanics who service the car – these all count. What is amazing is that the measures that then have to be taken to combat the climate change to which you have contributed – they count as well. The fun of driving and the disastrous effects of climate change *both* count because they cost money, and money has numbers on it and so can be counted.

So if there is to be an economy not driven by the idol of money, the first thing we need to do is change our view of how to count, and what should count, or, in other words, we need to change our view of what is the P in the GDP. That is because if it's only money value that counts as part of the product, and we're searching for growth, we really need to stop people doing DIY, stop the people who tend allotments and therefore buy less from the local greengrocer, stop people making Christmas presents instead of buying them, stop people, in short, doing anything that somebody might pay someone else to do. Nobody will admit to thinking that the world would be a better place if we stopped people doing all those worthy things – contributing to the *product* of a better, healthier, more wholesome world. That is, nobody admits to thinking that the only good things in the world are the things people are paid for, if you put the question to people in those terms. It is just that when we turn to economics we become the merciless number crunchers who only know how to count things if they have numbers on them.

This merciless economy has some particularly difficult aspects to it, concerned not so much with getting the weeding done, but something much more serious, that many thought had ceased to be a problem but, if recent reports are to be believed, has not. It seems that despite the legislation prescribing equal pay for women and men doing the same or equivalent jobs it has remained stubbornly the case women still receive considerably less in the workplace than men for doing even the same work. This seems to raise the question whether women working count less than men by the only value we have for counting things, which is money. For quite apart from the injustice which most would see in those differential pay rates, the reality is that more of the things that get done for money are done by men, and the things that women do they often do for no money at all; they spend a lot of time doing things that don't count towards the GDP.

More than men, by far, they bring up children; they care for elderly relatives; they are the backbone of most churches in the pastoral work they do for no money. Nobody is going to admit to believing that any of those things are unimportant, that they don't count – but nobody has found a way to count our GDP that takes these hugely important activities into account. And legislate as much as you will that women should be paid the same as men for equivalent work, the jobs that women do for money are in competition for their time and attention with jobs that they would be doing for nothing – the mothering, the volunteering and so forth. Because of that, women's labour will tend to be cheaper, a situation which our contemporary economy will tend to exploit without mercy. So if there is to be a merciful economy we shall need an economic system that stops counting and starts attending, or, to put it another way, one that acknowledges things count even if they don't have numbers in the form of pay scales. That seems to be a precondition for stopping merely talking about the valuable things women do and actually starting to value them.

The mercy of enough

We have referred early on in this exploration to the significance of the narrative of the flood in drawing the contrast between the world of the idols and the world as ruled by God. In Benjamin Britten's setting of the mystery play *Noye's Fludde* the entry of the animals two by two into the ark Noah had built before the onset of the deluge is accompanied by the repeated singing of *Kyrie, Kyrie, Kyrie eleison*. In this great entry the species of the animal creation capture centuries of liturgical introit processions in which the faithful and their ministers enter the sacred space, approaching the sanctuary with a plea for, and therefore a recognition of, the divine mercy. The music of the procession is confident: the divine mercy is not so much implored as it is celebrated, the utterly reliable characteristic of God which even as judgement looms will hold the universe in life, as is represented by including among the rescued a male and a female of each species.

The animals, with Noah's family, represent in themselves that firm divine commitment to continuity, held alongside an equally firm commitment to justice. God has seen that 'the wickedness of humankind was great in the earth, and that every inclination of the thoughts of their hearts was only evil continually' (Genesis 6.5). Yet God resolves nonetheless to provide *both* for the elimination of the humanity whose creation had become a source of divine grief, *and* for the continuity of the species, including the righteous Noah and his descendants.

The divine vengeance on human unrighteousness requires, it seems, little detailed planning: the waters of the deluge will take care of it, the violence and corruption of the earth engulfed in the chaos which is their inevitable outcome in a universe created by a moral God. What cannot be left simply to chaos and chance, however, is the merciful provision for continuity.

> 'Make yourself an ark of cypress wood; make rooms in the ark, and cover it inside and out with pitch. This is how you are to make it: the length of the ark three hundred cubits, its width fifty cubits, and its height thirty cubits. Make a roof for the ark, and finish it to a cubit above; and put the door of the ark in its side; make it with lower, second, and third decks.'
>
> (Genesis 6.14–16)

Mercy has an architecture, in this case a naval architecture with plans and a bill of quantities in conformity to building regulations. There can be no mercy without carpentry. That detailed instruction prefigures, after all, the art and architecture, the musical composition and execution, the liturgical structure and order that are necessary for Noah's successors to continue to celebrate God's utterly reliable mercy. Moreover, when the ark is ready it is specified, even in an account which avoids unnecessary detail, that survival rations require to be planned: 'Also, take with you every kind of food that is eaten, and store it up, and it shall serve as food for you and for them.' (Genesis 6.21)

Thus a deluge that is itself grounded not in the arbitrary outcomes of conflicts or love affairs between heavenly beings but in God's righteous demands is also the occasion of a mercy that is deliberate and detailed. So after the flood had abated the order of an abundant creation can be restored:

> God said to Noah, 'Go out of the ark, you and your wife, and your sons and your sons' wives with you. Take with you every living thing that is with you of all flesh – birds and animals and every creeping thing that creeps on the earth – so that they may abound on the earth, and be fruitful and multiply on the earth.'
>
> (Genesis 8.15–17)

More than that, the event which has cost so much destruction concludes with a commitment to the continuation of that mercy:

> And when the LORD smelt the pleasing odour [of Noah's sacrifice], the LORD said in his heart, 'I will never again curse the ground because of humankind, for the inclination of the human heart is evil from youth; nor will I ever again destroy every living creature as I have done. As long as the earth endures, seedtime and harvest, cold and heat, summer and winter, day and night, shall not cease.'
>
> (Genesis 8.21f.)

The morally ambiguous character of humanity is acknowledged; nonetheless there is established an abundant economy, not an economy of excess but one that has sufficient product of seedtime and harvest to sustain the world; the created order is redeemed from the arbitrariness of conflicts among deities and settled in

God's commitment to humankind despite its being a species acknowledged to have a 'heart that is evil from youth'. The mercy that saves a few in the ark is prelude to an all-embracing mercy that is God's universal and ultimately victorious purpose of salvation. The universal promise expressed in the rainbow set in the clouds is confirmed in Christ, his particular history establishing the sovereignty of mercy for the whole of creation.

> God waited patiently in the days of Noah for the building of the ark in which a few … were saved through water. And baptism, which this prefigured, now saves you … through the resurrection of Jesus Christ, who has gone into heaven and is at the right hand of God, with angels, authorities, and powers subject to him.
>
> (1 Peter 3.20–22)

Thus from their beginning to their end the Scriptures declare the pattern of the merciful economy. Yet to speak of 'economy', rather than use the gentler and theologically more fashionable term 'ecology', raises an unavoidable issue: what happens when this vision of the merciful purpose of God is brought into relation with the harsher realm of what we are accustomed to call 'the economy'? The vision of lions lying down with lambs is immediately attractive. But ultimately the beauty of this vision has to include much more difficult practical matters: the establishment of community between bosses and workers or between bankers and the poor of the earth. Even if the Bible sets out such a vision, the evidence of our time is that if all humankind has to proceed according to the ways of the governing economics there is little hope for comity among lambs and lions, or even grass and trees. Apart from comforting biblical pictures, could there be an *economics* of mercy, and what might it look like? What is its *architecture* to be? A merciful economy is not simply a matter of the right rhetoric; careful planning is needed if the ark is to float, and the vision has to be of an economy that on the one hand recognises the negative tendencies of the human heart without surrendering to them, while on the other living out a promise of sufficiency for all.

Planning for mercy

What cannot be in doubt following the crisis of 2008 and the years of flailing around for remedies that have followed is that a system ruled by money will not meet that challenge. It represents a total surrender to the corrupting tendencies of the human heart – in particular its tendency to fear and to greed – a reliance upon the idol of money in all its volatile, arbitrary and chaotic instability, in which the winners end up taking all and the losers lose yet more. As the sociologist of money, Nigel Dodd, puts it, in words that hint at the main point of this book's argument that money has become an idol:

> In the mature money economy, money's empowering features have compromised that very freedom which money itself promises to embrace. Monetary freedom has in this sense been alienating. It is a freedom which is empty of content, having only negative connotations linked to the removal of constraint … These life-contents will be stunted whenever money is treated as an end in itself. This is exactly what has happened in modern society. Money, as the ultimate economic instrument, has been turned into the ultimate economic goal. It has imploded in on itself as mammon.[2]

Fortunately, recent history is not lacking in examples of mercy-planning, where overriding demands for the survival of the vulnerable and the needs of the planet have led to political actions which have to a major extent put money in its place as instrument and denied its claims to sovereign rule, to empire, and above all as unchallengeable divinity overruling all other considerations and overwhelming with the sense of its being the sole refuge against disaster and the ultimate form of salvation.

Two examples will make the point: the last decades of the twentieth century saw the emergence of a large, ebullient and powerful movement for the relief of the unpayable debts of many of the poorest countries. The concept of *Jubilee* gained a place in many people's imagination, including many for whom biblical language and themes would not previously have counted for much. Not only was a highly successful campaign mobilised, but economic and political literacy, as well as some very significant theological understanding, took root. There were unforgettable events associated with the campaign, and they did have the result that significant amounts of unrepayable debt were remitted. Apocalyptic predictions of a total end to world trade if debts were not enforced were not fulfilled, and some quite unlikely politicians rushed to claim that they had always thought it a good thing to support. Ideas such as the need for national, rather than just personal, bankruptcy processes started to be openly discussed, significant amounts of debt were written off and the world seemed to entertain the vision, if fleeting and incomplete, that it was not necessary for nations to be permanently impoverished because of the economic system.

It was, with hindsight, the more radical and significant perceptions that were present in the campaign but took less root outside it that needed to be taken far more seriously than they were, and in particular that included the radical examination of money itself and the way it had operated to create the problem of unrepayable debt in the first place. Had that realisation received more attention the results of the debt remission campaign might have been more dramatic and longer lasting, and lessons might have carried over into the handling of the 2008 crisis and in particular its devastating effect on the poorest countries of the eurozone.

For what needed to be learned was that what had happened in terms of the impoverishment of nations was not a singular, let alone accidental, phenomenon but was intrinsic to the operation of the monetary system itself. Left to itself a market in money will produce the results we have experienced, first in the indebtedness of the poorest nations and second in the chaotic unravelling of the banking system as happened in the 2008 crisis and thereafter.

A further example of money being put in its place has to do with events in Germany following the end of the Soviet Union and the dismantling of the Berlin Wall, which made reunification possible. There was, inevitably, much debate about how the currencies of the former German Democratic Republic and the German Federal Republic were to be merged; that debate concluded with a recognition that neither the official East German rate of exchange, which would have required a West to East German mark exchange rate of 1:1, nor allowing the market to set the rate would work. The former would be too generous to be affordable, the latter would have impoverished citizens of the former East Germany, to the point, no doubt, of undermining faith in the possibility of reunion and even causing social unrest to break out. In the event citizens of the former GDR were given Deutschmarks at differential rates depending on the amount of money they had.

This is an outcome that quite clearly puts people and their needs before the rights of money itself, and made reunification possible. Again, the radical nature of that action was not spelled out. When the 2008 crisis hit the eurozone the German economy saw itself as making sacrifices for the sake of the poorest countries in the eurozone, while the poorest countries considered themselves to have had enormous burdens imposed on them.[3] Had the *meaning* of those earlier actions, of debt remission and of the differential exchange rates that accompanied German reunification, been much more widely expressed and understood as a decision not to let money rule, there might well have been a wider recognition of the accommodations that the eurozone crisis required.

For mercy requires planning, and a refusal to understand that leads to plans being rejected as 'state control' or else to the rejection of all planning, with the inevitable result that money is left in control, sovereign over governments and peoples, a power people can only quail before and seek to appease. If mercy in the days of Noah required architecture, the detailed survival planning which appears in the story of the flood, so also does the economy of mercy, the reining in of the power of money, require that human ingenuity is harnessed to plan for a system in which the power of money unrestrained is replaced by one that, while recognising the tendencies of the human heart, nonetheless makes provision for a future that is just and sustainable. The response to the devastation brought about by the chaotic and uncontrolled power of money has to be more than the rhetoric of unrestrained generosity; rather, it requires an architecture of mercy that contains the realism and the promise which combine in the biblical accounts.

In fact the years since the 2008 crisis have not been lacking in displays of that kind of ingenuity; there has been an enormous flurry of writing, parliamentary and other commissions have analysed the events that led to the crisis and made copious recommendations. There has been massive reorganisation, new regulations enforced – it is hoped – by new regulatory bodies. Promises of new corporate culture are made and repeated, and statements of good intention abound. 'Never again' has been said in response to the crisis – again and again.

But this frenetic activity does not amount to an economic architecture of mercy, rather a massive attempt at avoidance, for it would appear that all options are being explored other than the one thing needful, which is to consider mechanisms for the reining in of the power, the ubiquity and the status of money. This book has been an argument for considering that the ways in which money has been allowed to behave bear a very close resemblance to the behaviour of the ancient deities that the idols represented, whose chaotic, arbitrary and destructive ways were what the Hebrew peoples and their Christian successors also saw themselves as called to resist. Better banks, better regulated banks, a financial sector with a different culture, a stronger emphasis on long-term investment goals – these and the many other prescriptions that have been canvassed and, in some cases implemented, may well form part of the architecture of mercy, the detailed planning, that we shall need. But they will not effect the depth of change implied in the word 'mercy', that prioritising of the human, the just, the generous society, if the root of the problem in the power of money is not recognised.

The issue became very clear at an event recently sponsored by St Paul's Institute featuring Justin Welby, the Archbishop of Canterbury, himself a person experienced in the world of finance and a member of the Parliamentary Commission on Banking Standards, and the CEO of Barclays, Antony Jenkins. Barclays plc is an organisation which, under the leadership of its CEO, has engaged with cultural reform with the greatest seriousness. Jenkins spoke strongly about how determined he is to change the culture of his organisation from that which had brought not just Barclays but the whole sector into such serious disrepute.

He certainly showed that he knows the importance of the task he has undertaken. What has gone on at Barclays, not least in terms of rate-fixing, may have been – just – on the right side of the law; but most 'ordinary' people would think there was no doubt that what happened was very much on the wrong side of the line as far as morality is concerned. It is most unlikely that anybody will place trust in Barclays if it does not succeed in cleaning out its stable, and the culture to which Antony Jenkins aspires is without question a necessary condition for regaining trust, and even then that will only happen if it is not mere words but forms the basis for action.

What is more, there will have to be some sense that the words and the actions get somewhere near to the heart of the matter. It is important, of course, that far more transparent forms of accountability are put in place, alongside clear statements of what the policies are that will be counted as acceptable in the organisation. It is important as well to give some sense that longer-term aims are being given priority over short-term successes in the financial marketplace.

Those things matter. But so does the character of the incentives that are used in the organisation to encourage staff to work successfully and in accordance with the company's new-found ethos of transparency and probity. And here lies the most significant requirement: when it comes to incentives the medium is the message. The evidence is, sadly, that however determined Jenkins is to be an agent of change, he is still unable or unwilling to address the incentives issue. In the early months of 2014 it became clear that he was not going – at least not yet – to let the message of a new culture determine the medium of incentives. He advanced a public defence of the enormous Barclays bonus pool: there was no sign of change there. The bonuses were going to be massive – as before – and the money numbers were pretty eye-watering to most of the listeners. From what he said it did not sound as though Jenkins found them so or was particularly sensitive to how they would sound.

And the arguments hadn't changed either. 'We have to pay these bonuses because other people do, and they are our competitors.' 'If we don't pay the rates that good people can command in the market we'll lose them and we won't be able to make a success of this business.' Even if we pass over the awkward question whether all these 'good' people were quite that good (given where they took us in 2008) and the unexamined assumption about what 'goodness' is involved here, the question remains: can he be unaware that it is precisely the lure of such financial rewards that brings people into the industry who have huge ambitions towards the making of money? Can that be good for the industry in the long term?[4]

The individual people involved are doubtless good in all sorts of ways – not least in their personal lives, with their children, and even, we may hope, in the communities they inhabit and sometimes in the philanthropic generosity they can display. But as we have argued earlier, good people are no less vulnerable to being formed by Mammon and deflected from true ethical standards by the mesmerising effects of large numbers. And the real problem with money is that (if what the Christian faith says about it is true) it is extremely difficult to combine the service of Mammon with a real willingness to prioritise the justice and hope that are the hallmarks of God's commonwealth. The warning about the difficulty a camel faces confronted with the eye of a needle is not simply about 'spiritual wellbeing' but about life in the real world, the real Barclays – and the other 'real' corporate enterprises. If money in those quantities is what is used as the primary incentive, then money will remain as the primary measure of achievement, and will trump all other measures. The medium is the message, and any new ethical culture will be quite ineffective if it is not grounded in a serious address to the dominance of money.

We should notice, too, that 'incentives' are not only the positive ones of bonuses and high salaries. These are incentive *rewards*. But what has emerged from the crisis is another form of financial incentive too, and that is financial *punishment*. The period since 2008 has been marked in our society by a powerful rhetoric of punishment directed not at those whose actions played a significant part in the crisis but rather at those who are the poorest. Under the guise of 'welfare reform' and the weasel language of 'helping people into work' – and the people being 'helped' include some seriously disabled – we hear groups spoken of as 'trapped on benefit', when in fact for some of them the benefits they have received have been their only means of survival. This is without question the language of financial punishment, the mark of a society in which the huge rewards received by some are matched by punitive responses to the most vulnerable. It is a long way from a merciful economy.

The benefit of mercy

As was observed in Chapter 6, if money has acquired the marks of an idol, a divinity extending its power over all areas of life, it will form its devotees, their values and their inner life. As this revealed itself in characteristics deriving from money's quantitative expansion, its volatility and distractedness, so also the way in which money deals routinely in enormous rewards and devastating punishments infects society more widely with a mentality that regards rewarding and punishing as the default way in which human beings are to treat one another. Threatening becomes the most usual way in which to get people to fall into line; the threats may not be financial ones, but they are characteristic of the reward and punishment mentality which tends to afflict a society dominated by financial considerations. An exuberant group of young people causing a disturbance is likely to be threatened rather than appealed to; posters asking for people to license their televisions are full of threats of detector vans and the fines that will be imposed on the owners of unlicensed televisions, not with invitations to people to consider their enjoyment of television programmes and the need for all who enjoy them to make a contribution to the costs of programming.

This latter example is an instance of the way in which one of the most potent instruments we have at our disposal for implementing an economy of mercy, namely taxation, is bedevilled by the constant intrusion of language derived from money's overriding tendency to encourage the mentality of rewards and punishments. So taxation needs to be commended not just as one way of enabling fair assessment of the contributions we can make to the public services we all need; it also puts money in its place, interrupting its tendency to enhance the social stresses which inequality creates and to determine a person's rights and status. Instead, the language of 'the taxpayer' and 'the licence fee payer' is used all too often in political discourse to express demands and rights over others.

Given what we know about the damaging effects of ever increasing inequality, the suggestion of a 'citizen income', a basic income for all, offers real possibilities for solidarity and an end to the complexities of housing benefit and welfare payments, means testing and allowances. Implementing the architecture of such a citizen income would of course require much detailed debate and planning; the point here, however, is that what prevents such discussion even starting is the assumption, which will be voiced very early in the conversation, that if people were not rewarded for working and punished for not doing so nobody would work. Usually those who voice such sentiments would reply negatively if asked whether their only reason for working is that it is financially rewarded; but the belief persists that 'people generally' only respond to rewards and punishments. Thus the pattern of thought that money encourages dominates political discussion and moral attitudes.

Yet we know that there are more creative ways for human beings to behave towards one another than by rewards and punishments. In the matter of personal wrong, there comes a point in the nursing of a grudge, in holding on to a grievance, when the question arises, 'Is this doing any good?' Being able to move on is frequently about reaching the point of recognition that being in the right is not in fact sufficient. A failure to move into the mode of mercy simply means that the grievance, however legitimate, possesses the aggrieved person more than it brings any repentance or recompense from the guilty one. Whole nations and parts of nations manifest this very point; unfortunately the apprehension of this element of self-interest and advantage in surrendering a grievance can take a great deal of time to achieve.

There is a precise parallel with what is enabled to happen when money is not allowed to have the last word. The merciless economy dominated by the power of money parallels the merciless economy of retained grievance. The illusion of the money economy is that of 'financial discipline', of figures in ledgers, of keeping accounts. The economy of grievance presents the same illusion: 'scores' of wrongs are kept – and settled. Crimes are allocated 'tariffs'; and criminals therefore accounted to have a 'debt to society'.

Held in place by a larger vision of human community, the disciplines of accounting have their place. Within such a vision, proper charges and repayments can all give stability and security to relationships, upholding fairness in commercial transactions and encouraging a measure of responsibility. Such is true in the economy of all social relations, not only, but not least, those described as 'economic'. Unregulated and unchecked, however, detached from accountability to a wider vision of the human community and thus themselves accountable to nothing and nobody, the ledger accounts, whether of money or of wrongs, serve only themselves and feed on themselves. The economy of mercy, on the other hand, is a vision of humanity in which money is a discipline that can once again serve our common life, not a sovereign to rule us, nor an emperor bestriding the world, nor a divinity expecting our worship and sacrifice, determining our values and prescribing our vision.

Not gambling on chaos but trusting in the practice of mercy, we shall have an economy for planetary sustainability and human flourishing, truly a household to share. It will be guided by qualities, not ruled by numbers; it will have the flexibility of remission and the generosity of attention to need. It will share in the commitment of the rainbow in the sky, one that no negative response will negate and no passage of time make obsolete. It will share in the mercy of God.

Notes

[1] This chapter includes a substantial adaptation of a paper first given in 2000 to the Society for the Study of Theology. See my 'The Merciful Economy' in Alistair McFadyen and Marcel Sarot (eds.), *Forgiveness and Truth* (T&T Clark, 2001), pp. 99ff., quoted by permission of Bloomsbury Publishing plc.

[2] Nigel Dodd, *The Sociology of Money: Economics, Reason and Contemporary Society* (Continuum, 1994), p. 49.

3   See Chapter 4 above for comments on the situation facing Cyprus and
    Greece.

4   For a fuller account of the event at which the Archbishop and Antony
    Jenkins discussed 'Good banks', see *The City and the Common Good*, http://
    stpaulsinstitute.org.uk/reports; for the full article on which these reflections
    are based, see http://www.stpaulsinstitute.org.uk/dialogue/peter-selby/
    opinion/2014/mar/19/peter-selby/opinion/2014/mar/19/money-
    ethical-issue-jenkins

9

Faith in the economy

As this exploration draws to its close it is right to ask what kind of exploration this has been. After all, given how fashionable it has become to think and write about money and what has happened to it, this might be an essay to add to that section of the bookcase: it can be reckoned another description of what has happened to money and, in that context, what has happened to us who use it. The evaluation of those developments has been critical, even negative, about what has happened to money and what changes that has brought about in human life: the argument has been that because money has grown so much in quantity and speed of transmission it has also acquired massive power over the way we think and live.

Money doesn't just talk, it rules. And it doesn't just rule at home, but worldwide. Many passages in this book can be read to say that what money has done is to claim all the power and authority in human affairs: it has abolished frontiers by having no respect for them and making national currencies and governmental control of them subject to a market in money which is far outside the capacity of governments to control. If they cannot buck the market, and if money rules, then governments are on the verge of becoming helpless pawns in a game whose rules are made by the way money works and whose winners are those with the largest stakes to wager. They will ensure that to those who have will be given more: they reward themselves highly even when they fail.

So the hard-won democratic privilege, the suffrage which makes all equal in making the law and in conforming to it, has been subverted. No longer a protection for the poor against the machinations of the well resourced and the well armed, it has been able to seduce the majority into believing and behaving as those who believe that the well-being of society and of themselves and their families is best served by going along with the wishes of the powerful and the wealthy; money has enabled the subversion of desire so that it is the moneyed who are protected from the ambitions of the poor, for the poor have come to believe that only in the richness of the rich lies any hope for them that some crumbs might fall from the table.

Furthermore, if all this is so, the poor are right not to rest their hopes on making plans, pursuing ambitions and engaging in work, because society is not any longer arranged to serve their needs. Their best hope is to gamble on the small chance that they too could be winners – since a small chance is, even so, better than no chance at all: to buy a lottery ticket is the sensible act of the person for whom it is the only conceivable way of being transformed from being a loser to being a winner. Most of the proceeds of the purchases of lottery tickets and scratch cards will, after the prizes have been paid, go to enhance the profits of the organisers: a bookmaker has to be very unlucky or incompetent to lose. Furthermore, the gambling choice says something very significant about what money has been revealed to be, namely the agent of chaos. Life does not just enable the activity of gambling; fundamentally it *is* a gamble. We saw that in 2008, when it all fell to pieces; but we can see it anyway when we read what the 'advisers' tell us we need to do in order to secure a reasonably resourced old age, where to put your money to the greatest effect. And what we see is that the system only works because the 'experts' disagree with each other, and the poor punter – rightly so called – has to guess and hope that he or she has made the right guess. If all the 'experts' agreed there could be no winners.

And finally, money, the argument has run, has taken us to the edge of disaster, not just because the economic system came near to collapse but because it depends to a huge extent on debt, and debt is using tomorrow's resources (assuming you will have some) today. Among tomorrow's resources are not just your own sources of income but are also, and most importantly, the resources within the life of the planet to sustain life into the future. When in justification for policies to 'reduce the deficit' politicians speak of not leaving a debt to be paid by succeeding generations they are saying more than they want us to notice: what will fall to be paid is not just money. They will be faced with a far more serious deficit, a deficit of the natural resources which our living on debt-based money has consumed. There are more significant things on the verge of running out than the money in the economy: what money is making us use up are the very necessities of life, along with what might not be thought necessary (in that you can stay alive without some of it) but adds hugely to life's richness within the diversity and beauty of the world.

If such is the reading of this book's argument, then it is joined to the large number of writings which have sought to warn and to campaign. Since the crisis of 2008 the number of such writings has increased and, encouragingly, so has the willingness of authors to make the kinds of connections that have appeared in earlier chapters. And beyond writing, there has been significant action also: the members of Greenpeace, churches inviting us to 'Shrink the Footprint', Operation Noah, Friends of the Earth – these and many others would, we could hope, find in these pages some arguments in support, and perhaps even some elements of a diagnosis, which connect the danger in which we stand with the economic system as we have allowed it to develop.

If the argument is read in that way, then the space devoted to biblical citation, to making the contrast between the gods of the ancient pantheon and the God of the Hebrew people, the God confessed as the Father of Jesus Christ, and the one whom Christian believers worship, has perhaps some value as inspiration to those to whom that language is important but does not fundamentally add to the argument. That there are similarities between the attributes of the ancient gods and the behaviour of money in our time is perhaps interesting, but the economic points are essentially 'secular', based on the evidence gained from observing the world we inhabit now and a consideration of the history of the development of money. To put it with the bluntness with which Bishop David Jenkins, sometime Bishop of Durham, was accustomed to express himself, the theological material in this book is on that reading no more than 'the kind of God-talk which people who use God-talk use

to talk to people who use God–talk'. For those who do not it may
be of passing anthropological interest to know how a Christian
theologian might approach this topic, but no more.

It is possible, on the other hand, to read the argument in
exactly the opposite way. That is, it would be possible to see
this argument as seeking to engage the reader's sympathy for
the continued use of terms like 'idol' and 'deity' by showing the
relationship between those terms and some elements in the way the
world economy has developed. There would be an element here of
seeking to rehabilitate a term such as idol, to restore something of
its original sense in a world where it has little left to it beyond being
a colloquial expression to describe a celebrity – as in 'Hollywood
idol'. In the process, on that reading, the predominant concern is
not to make a political and economic point about money but to
make what theologians would call an *apologetic* point, to *commend*
some significant biblical insights as having a meaning which can be
illustrated by reference to what has happened to the economy. The
book would then have succeeded in its aim if readers were able
to see the connection between what 'idol' means and an aspect of
contemporary living, and to acknowledge that the word has as a
result some significant resonances. But just as in the case of the other
reading of the argument, where it appeared that the theological
material was evocative, perhaps, but did not add significantly to
the main economic agenda, so on this reading the material about
money might serve to *illustrate* the meaning of the traditions about
God and the idols, but would not fundamentally *add* to it.

These two possible readings of the book's argument are
described in this way so as to clarify the point that neither reading
of the material is completely accurate to the book's intention, but
both contain elements of importance that are to be found within it.
The matter goes to the heart of the relationship between religious
and secular views of the world, whether they complement each
other or are inevitably totally opposed to each other.

That issue was highlighted in 2012 when Professor Michael
Sandel addressed a meeting at St Paul's Cathedral on the occasion
of the launch of the British edition of his *What Money Can't Buy:
The Moral Limits of Markets*. He had made a presentation and as part

of the panel responding to that I observed that the book was in effect 'a secular warning against idolatry'. In further conversation, Michael Sandel responded, 'You say my book is a "secular warning against idolatry"; I accept that, and would suggest that that shows that the connection and relation between secular and religious views of the world are more fluid than we sometimes suppose.'[1]

The question is, of course, what we mean by a relation that is 'more fluid than we sometimes suppose'. Does it mean that at least sometimes the secular and religious viewpoints coincide exactly? Or does it mean that they are different but have significant overlaps. In the context of the argument of this book, does showing that some of the ways in which money now behaves are analogous to, or similar to, or echo – the choice of word might be significant – the behaviour attributed in the ancient texts to the idols and the deities they represent *add* anything to the information we have about money? Or does it simply present it in an evocative way for those who respond to that kind of historical information? Or, on the hand,(if the argument is correct), does the knowledge that there are such analogies or echoes or similarities between the way in which the ancient deities were believed to behave and the way we observe money to behave in the economy *add* anything to what we know about the characteristics of the ancient deities?

This book is written in the conviction that pointing to these analogies, echoes or similarities is more than a useful device for illustrating either the attributes of deities or the behaviour of money in the economy, but does in fact *add* to what we are able to say about both. Yet Sandel's comment about the boundary between two perceptions being more fluid than we sometimes suppose is important in preparing us to recognise that the relationship between the two perceptions is not one of the simple opposition that many debates between avowed atheists and avowed believers may suggest. But his comment also leaves room for the possibility at the same time that the perceptions do not exactly coincide, and that in either direction something additional may be supplied to the one by the other.

How does that apply in this case? What does it add to our critique of the nature and behaviour of money to introduce the discussion of the behaviour of the ancient deities? And equally, does it add anything to our understanding of idolatry if we can see the beliefs to which we give that title being acted out in relation to money?

In our examination of money one of the things that became clear is that money was acting in a *formative* way in relation to our lives. It had moved beyond the functions for which it exists to the exercise of a pervasive influence on what we feel, what we think and what we do. The whole point of our critique is that money has succeeded, because of the developments that have occurred in its nature, in inserting itself into every corner of our existence. What that amounts to is the acquisition by money of the capacity to alter our concept of the direction and meaning of life, what are its possibilities and dangers. The whole point about what has happened to money is not just that it has intruded itself into so many different areas of our lives one by one, but that it has staged a takeover of the issue of purpose, that in its ubiquity it has entered the religious arena simply by the range of its intrusions. The history of money may be one of steady accretion, but we now wake up to find the totality of its coverage of our lives.

As to the way the argument works in the other direction, what I have said about idols and their worship in the ancient world is very common knowledge, and in itself probably adds nothing to what many if not most believers already know. But connecting the world view in which they figure with the world of money is not simply *illustrative*, a way of conveying with a contemporary picture what it might have been like to be part of a world in which such deities figure; it also makes that point that those who recorded – and railed against and sung about – the conflict between God and the deities believed that they were discussing something of cosmic and enduring significance that could reappear as an issue precisely in the specific challenges of a later age. Hence what the observations about money add to any prior knowledge about idols: that they were thought to be dangerous because they had the capacity in principle to intrude into any situation that might later develop. Thus the issues around justice and concern for the vulnerable which were God's especial care can be expected to appear again in opposition to other more immediate strategies for dealing with the challenges facing society and individuals.

My comment on Michael Sandel's presentation, and his book, that it is a 'secular warning against idolatry' was intended to make the positive point that he identifies with great accuracy the points at which money is intruding where it does not belong, and to appreciate, from the point of view of a believer, having had put before me all those indications of what happens when money takes over in the way that it has. But I also believe that there is an important point to make to someone who seeks to critique money in purely secular terms: namely that allowing 'idol' to be a term of economics alerts us to the range, the height, the depths of money's intrusion and, more important still, that to speak of 'God' is to speak of an economy profoundly different from what money might offer, however much of it you have. For what the people have learned who have spoken of God and of Jesus Christ – often through their failures of obedience – is that the only safe ground on which to build an economy is the mercy in which our ancestors found they could place their trust. To rely on anything else brings with it the chaos and oppression associated with the idols, and leads – has often and very recently led, and could well lead sooner than we think – to the shaking of earth's very foundations.

Just as the text of this book neared completion, there took place in London a remarkable, large conference under the title 'Inclusive Capitalism'. It might be judged in itself a sign of hope that a conference with such a title could even happen. In the course of it the Governor of the Bank of England, Mark Carney, delivered a speech which included some trenchant critiques of the direction which unregulated capitalism has taken in recent decades, a number of them similar to points made in earlier chapters of this book. He began, however, with this very positive observation, a ground for hope that there might indeed be a desire for the common good that is more widespread than is often supposed:

> Societies aspire to this trinity of distributive justice, social equity and intergenerational equity for at least three reasons. First, there is growing evidence that relative equality is

good for growth. At a minimum, few would disagree that a society that provides opportunity to all of its citizens is more likely to thrive than one which favours an elite, however defined. Second, research suggests that inequality is one of the most important determinants of relative happiness and that a sense of community – itself a form of inclusion – is a critical determinant of well-being. Third, they appeal to a fundamental sense of justice. Who behind a Rawlsian veil of ignorance – not knowing their future talents and circumstances – wouldn't want to maximise the welfare of the least well off?[2]

He makes clear that meeting such aspirations requires detailed and concrete actions with many links to what was described in the last chapter as the 'architecture of mercy', technically complex but with an aim in which Carney describes, in similarly secular terms to those used by Sandel, a remaking of finance as servant rather than ruler.

If Sandel is right in asserting that the boundary between secular and religious commentary is more fluid than we often suppose, then it is also true that the boundary between secular hopes – represented in Carney's speech – and religious faith might be similarly porous. This theological critique of money has sought to establish that an understanding of the traditions of idolatry adds enormous depth and range to the observations many have made about what money has been allowed to become and the range of the disasters to which that can lead. It does that while adding weight to the contention that the struggles of our ancestors against the idols have again and again to be repeated when new idols appear.

But such a theological critique shows something else too: reflecting on the range and scope of money's intrusions into areas of life in which it does not belong reveals possibilities for change and for the realisation of the widespread aspiration towards an inclusive economy. The actions that might be required – of the kind Carney describes – are indeed specific and technical, as the 'merciful economy' that is the alternative to rule by the idol that money has become needs to be worked out precisely in each generation and situation. But what the theological critique also reveals by examining the confrontation with the idols in days of old is the depth and length and breadth and height of the enduring mercy that faith discerns as the hope of the world. And for all of us – since all of us find ourselves engaging with money alongside questions of life's ultimate meaning – that must be good news.

Notes

1. The full event can be heard as a podcast: see http://audioboo.fm/boos/1920004-what-money-can-t-buy-michael-sandel-speaks-at-st-paul-s-cathedral-2012. See Michael Sandel, *What Money Can't Buy* (Penguin, 2012) for his critique of the 'moral limits of markets'.
2. Mark Carney at 'Inclusive Capitalism' conference, 3 June 2014. See www.bankofengland.co.uk/publications/Pages/speeches/default.aspx.

Bibliography

Ackerman, Susan, 'Idol, Idolatry' in Freedman, David Noel (ed.), *Eedrmans Dictionary of the Bible* (Eerdmans, 2000)

Ahmad, Khurshid (ed.), *Eliminating Riba from the Economy* (Institute of Policy Studies, Islamabad, 1994)

Ahmad, Ziauddin et al. (eds.), Money and Banking in Islam (Institute of Policy Studies, Islamabad, 1983)

Atherton, John, *Christianity and the Market* (SPCK, 1992)

Atherton, John, Baker, Chris and Reader, John, *Christianity and the New Social Order* (SPCK, 2011)

Barnet, Richard and Cavanagh, John, 'Electronic Money and the Casino Economy' in Edward Goldsmith and Jerry Mander (eds.), *The Case Against the Global Economy* (Earthscan, 2001), pp. 58–69.

Bartholomew, James, *The Welfare State We're In* (Politico's, 2004)

Beale, G. K., *We Become What We Worship* (InterVarsity Press, 2008)

Benedict XVI, Pope, *Caritas in Veritate* (Vatican Press, 2009)

Benston, George I, *Regulating Financial Markets* (IEA, 1998)

Bishop, Matthew and Green, Michael, *The Road from Ruin* (A&C Black, 2011)

Boyle, Nicholas, *Who Are We Now?* (Continuum, 2000)

Bruegemann, Walter, *Genesis* (Westminster John Knox Press, 1986)
— *Hopeful Imagination* (SCM Press, 1986)

Cobb, John, Jr, *The Earthist Challenge to Economism* (Macmillan, 1999)

De Gruchy, John W., *Christianity and Democracy* (Cambridge University Press, 1995)

Dent, M. J., *Jubilee 2000* (M. J. Dent, 1994)

De Santa Ana, Julio, *Good News to the Poor* (WCC, 1977)

Doctrine Commission, 'Money' in *Being Human* (Church House Publications, 2004), pp 55ff.

Dodd, Nigel, *The* Sociology of Money (Continuum, 1994)

Dominy, Peter, *Decoding Mammon* (Wipf & Stock, 2012)

Duchrow, Ulrich, *Alternatives to Global Capitalism* (International Books and Kairos Europa, 1995)

Dudley, Rebecca and Jones, Linda (eds.), *Turn the Tables* (CAFOD, 2003)

El Diwany, Tarek, *The Problem with Interest* (Kreatoc, 2010)

Evans, C. F., *St Luke* (SCM Press, 1990)

Evans, C. F., *The Lord's Prayer* (SCM Press, reprint 1997)

Featherby, James, *Of Markets and Men* (Tomorrow's Company, 2012)

Ferguson, Niall, *The Ascent of Money* (Allen Lane, 2008)

Francis, Pope, *Evangelii Gaudium* (Vatican Press, 2013)

Galbraith, John Kenneth, *The Culture of Contentment* (Sinclair-Stephenson, 1992)

Gardiner, Geoffrey, *Towards True Monetarism* (Dulwich Press, 1993)

George, Susan, *The Debt Boomerang* (Pluto Press, 1992)

George, Susan, *A Fate Worse than Debt* (Penguin, 1998)

George, Susan & Sabelli, Fabrizio, *Faith and Credit* (Penguin, 1994)

Gold, Gerry and Feldman, Paul, *A House of Cards* (Lupus, 2007)

Goldsmith, Edward and Mander, Jerry, *The Case Against the Global Economy* (Earthscan, 2001)

González, Justo L., *Faith and Wealth* (SCM Press, 2007)

Goodchild, Philip, *Theology of Money* (Harper & Row, 1977)

Gorringe, Timothy, *Capital and the Kingdom* (SPCK, 1994)

Goudzwaard, Bob and de Lange, Harry, *Beyond Poverty and Affluence* (Eerdmans & WCC, 1991)

Graeber, David, *Debt: The First 5000 Years* (Melville House, 2011)

Grau, Marion, *Of Divine Economy: Redefining Redemption* (T&T Clark, 2004)

Green, Stephen, *Serving God, Serving Mammon* (Marshall Pickering, 1996)

Green, Stephen, *Good Value* (Allen Lane, 2009)

Harries, Richard, *Is There a Gospel for the Rich?* (Mowbray, 1992)

Harrison, Fred, *The Traumatised Society* (Shepheard-Walwyn, 2012)

Hartropp, Andrew, *The Debt Trap* (Jubilee Centre, 1988)

Heslam, Peter, *Globalization: Unravelling the New Capitalism* (Grove Books, 2002)

Hilary, John, *The Poverty of Capitalism* (Pluto Press, 2013)

Hill, Octavia, *Homes of the London Poor* (Dodo Press Reprint, original 1875)

Huber, Joseph and Robertson, James, *Creating New Money* (New Economics Foundation, 2000)

Hutton, Will, *The State We're In* (Vintage Books, 1995)

Jackson, Kevin, *The Oxford Book of Money* (Oxford University Press, 1996)

Jenkins, David, *Market Whys and Human Wherefores* (Cassell, 2000)

Khor, Martin, *Rethinking Globalization* (Zed Books, 2001)

Logan, Pat, *A World Transformed* (CTBI, 2007)

Luther, Martin, *Large Catechism* (1580) in Theodore G. Tappert (ed.), *The Book of Concord* (Fortress Press, 1959)

McLeay, Michael, Radia, Amar and Thomas, Ryland, 'Money Creation in the modern economy', Bank of England Quarterly Bulletin, 2014/1 See www.bankofengland.co.uk/publications/Documents/quarterlybulletin/2014/qb14q102.pdf)

McLeod, George F., *Money: A Christian View. First Report of the Christian Doctrine of Wealth Committee* (Congregational Union of Scotland, 1963)

Marquand, David, *Mammon's Kingdom: An Essay on Britain, Now* (Allen Lane, 2014)

Martin, Felix, *Money: The Unauthorised Biography* (Bodley Head, 2013)

National Consumer Council, *Credit and Debt: The Consumer Interest* (HMSO, 1990)

Novak, Michael, *The Spirit of Democratic Capitalism* (Simon & Schuster, 1982)

Oakman, Douglas E., *Jesus and the Economic Questions of His Day* (Edwin Mellow Press, 1986)

Piketty, Thomas, *Capital in the Twenty-First Century* (Belknap Press, 2014)

Preston, Ronald, *Religion and the Ambiguities of Capitalism* (SCM Press, 1991)

Robertson, James, *Future Money: Breakdown or Breakthrough* (Green Books, 2012)

Rowbotham, Michael, *The Grip of Death* (Jon Carpenter, 1998)

Sachs, Jeffrey, *The End of Poverty* (Penguin, 2005)

Sacks, Jonathan, *Morals and Markets* (Institute of Economic Affairs, 1998)

Sandel, Michael, *What Money Can't Buy: The Moral Limits of Markets* (Penguin, 2012)

Selby, Peter, *Grace and Mortgage: The Language of Faith and the Debt of the World* (Darton, Longman & Todd, 1997/2009)

Selby, Peter, 'The Merciful Economy' in McFadyen, Alistair and Sarot, Marcel (eds.), *Forgiveness and Truth* (T&T Clark, 2001), pp. 99ff.

Selby, Peter, 'The Silent Word Still Speaks' in Reed, Charles (ed.), *Development Matters* (Church House, 2001), pp. 97ff.

Selby, Peter, 'Trading in Debt' in Dudley, Rebecca and Jones, Linda (eds.), *Turn the Tables* (CAFOD, 2003), pp.15–18

Selby, Peter, 'Reigning from the Tree', presidential address (Society for the Study of Theology, 2003)

Selby, Peter, 'Freedom from the Body of Death' in Watson, Natalie and Burns, Stephen (eds.), *Exchanges of Grace* (SCM Press, 2008), pp. 92ff.

Selby, Peter, *Structures of Disdain*, the Gore lecture 2006 (see http://westminster-abbey.org)

Selby, Peter, *Misestablishment*, the Eric Symes Abbott Lecture 2012 (see http://westminster-abbey.org)

Shakespear, Rodney and Challen, Peter, *Seven Steps to Justice* (New European Publications, 2002)

Skidelsky, Robert and Skidelsky, Edward, *How Much Is Enough? Money and the Good* Life (Other Press, 2012)

Taylor, Michael, *Poverty and Christianity* (SCM Press, 2000)

Temple, William, *Christianity and Social Order* (Penguin, 1942)

Ucko, Hans, *The Jubilee Challenge: Utopia or Possibility* (WCC, 1997)

Van Drimmelen, Rob, *Faith in a Global Economy* (WCC, 1997)

Warburton, Peter, *Debt and Delusion* (Allen Lane, 1999)

Ward, Barbara and Dubos, René, *Only One Earth* (Penguin, 1971)

Wilkinson, Richard and Pickett, Kate (Penguin, 2009)

Williams, Rowan, *Faith in the Public Square* (Bloomsbury, 2012)

Wilson, Rodney, *Economics, Ethics and Reason* (Macmillan, 1997)

Wink, Walter, *The Powers that Be* (Doubleday, 1998)

Yoder, John Howard, *The Politics of Jesus* (Eerdmans, 1994)

DARTON·LONGMAN+TODD

WESTMINSTER FAITH DEBATES

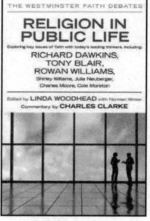

978-0-232-53018-6
£8.99 - Out now!

978-0-232-53019-3
£8.99 - Due Oct 2014

These unique books are distilled from the Westminster Faith Debates on *Religion in Public Life* and *Religion and Personal Life*, and outline the views of leading thinkers and policy makers including Alastair Campbell, Polly Toynbee, Giles Fraser, Delia Smith. Richard Dawkins, Tony Blair and Rowan Williams.

Designed with Religious Studies students in mind, they present the arguments of each speaker and a summary of each debate, followed by questions to prompt further reflection and discussion, and relevant statistics and resources.

The Westminster Faith Debates are organised by former Home Secretary Charles Clarke and Professor Linda Woodhead.

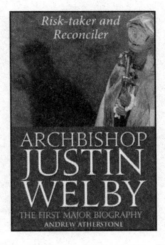